Mastering MacBook Air 2025 (M4)

From

Beginner To Pro

The Complete Guide to Seamless Setup, Pro Tips, Hidden Tricks, Troubleshooting, and Unlocking Advanced Features for Maximum Performance

Kai J. Tempest

Mastering Unreal Engine 5 from Beginner to Pro: The Definitive Guide to Building High-Quality Games, Immersive Virtual Worlds, and Advanced Interactive Contents.

First edition. April 2025.

Written by Kai J. Tempest

CONTENTS

INTRODUCTION TO THE MACBOOK AIR 2025 WITH M4 CHIPS

The MacBook Air 2025 is crafted for everyday excellence, catering to a diverse range of users—from students and professionals to tech enthusiasts. This guide is your key to unlocking the full potential of your new device, making it easy to master its features and functionality with confidence.

We start with the basics, ensuring that even those new to Mac can set up their MacBook Air effortlessly. You'll become acquainted with its sleek design, powerful performance, and the innovations that set the 2025 model apart from its predecessors.

This comprehensive guide goes beyond initial setup. It delves into advanced features and offers practical advice for optimizing your MacBook Air's performance. You'll learn how to customize your device to fit your personal or professional needs, harnessing the power of macOS for an enhanced user experience.

Whether you are transitioning from a different laptop or moving up from an older MacBook, our book is structured to make your adaptation process smooth and intuitive. We cover everything from daily operations to advanced functions, ensuring you gain the skills and knowledge to utilize your MacBook Air effectively.

By the end of this guide, you will be proficient in using your MacBook Air, confident in navigating its features, and equipped to handle everyday tasks with ease. This book is designed to be a valuable resource, making your journey with the MacBook Air 2025 both enjoyable and productive.

MACBOOK AIR 2025

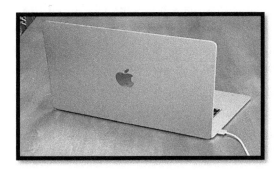

The MacBook Air 2025 is a sleek and lightweight laptop designed with both style and performance in mind. Known for its thin profile and long battery life, it's the ideal choice for anyone who needs a reliable device for work, study, or entertainment. With the latest M4 chip, the MacBook Air 2025 offers fast processing speeds, making it capable of handling everything from browsing the web to running more demanding applications. Its Retina display delivers clear and vibrant visuals, perfect for watching videos or editing photos. Plus, the MacBook Air is built to be energy-efficient, ensuring you get through your day without constantly needing to recharge. This guide will help you get the most out of your MacBook Air, making it easier to navigate and enjoy all the features this powerful laptop has to offer. The M3 MacBook Air from Apple has finally become a part of the Mac range, but the M4 MacBook Air is already in the works. Apple surprised us with the release of the M4 chip in the iPad Pro in early May, barely six months after the M3 debuted in the MacBook Pro. These are the specs for the chip as announced:

Models with 256GB or 512GB of storage

- 9-core CPU (3 performance cores and 6 efficiency cores)
- 10-core GPU
- Hardware-accelerated ray tracing
- 16-core Neural Engine
- 120GB/s memory bandwidth
- 8GB RAM

Models with 1TB or 2TB storage

- 10-core CPU (4 performance cores and 6 efficiency cores)
- 10-core GPU
- Hardware-accelerated ray tracing
- 16-core Neural Engine
- 120GB/s memory bandwidth

- 16GB RAM

The M4 has two more efficient cores than the 8-core M3, and it can handle more memory (120 GB/s vs. 100 GB/s). Most likely, Apple will use the same design for the Mac. This makes the M4 the first chip that isn't a Pro or Max with Before the M4 chip got into the iPad, it was said that it would focus on making AI better. During its Let Loose event, Apple quickly talked about the improved Neural Engine and how it can handle more than 38 trillion operations per second. However, the company didn't go into much detail about how this would be used in the real world. The WWDC keynote and the launch of the iPhone 16 with the A18 chip are expected to have a lot more to say about AI.

M4 MacBook Air: Design and Specs

This is not the fourth time that the current MacBook Air design has been updated with an M4 chip. Instead, it is the fourth version of the M-series chip in the MacBook Air. When Apple released the M1 MacBook Air in 2020, it had an older design that worked with Intel chips. The new design didn't come out until July 2022, when the M2 chip change was released. It's not likely that Apple will change it at all for the M4. With the M3 update in March 2025, Apple made a small change to the style of the Air, but it was only for one color. The Midnight model now has an anodization seal that helps keep fingerprints from showing up. This is a similar process that was added to the Space Black MacBook Pro. It's not likely that Apple will offer the process for Silver, Space Gray, and Starlight. Mark Gurman said in April that Apple might raise the maximum amount of memory that its high-end desktop Macs, which have more powerful M-series chips, can hold. If the M4 has better AI features, it might need more memory, no matter what level of M4 it is. But Apple might decide that the base M4 won't get more memory to keep costs down and get people to think about buying a higher-level device. The energy life is another thing that is improved. If the MacBook M4's chip is designed like the iPad Pro's, it might use less energy because it would have two extra saving cores. Maybe that will make the battery last longer.

If you add an M4 update, the MacBook Air will probably stay the same in every other way. Wi-Fi, Bluetooth, the camera, mics, speakers, ports, and display should all stay the same.

Target Audience and Typical Use Cases

The M4 chip in the MacBook Air is meant to appeal to a wide range of users, but it's mostly aimed at those who need a balance between speed, portability, and efficiency. There are a few main groups that can be used to describe the target audience. Each of these groups has unique needs that the MacBook Air can meet.

Target Audience

- o **Students and Educators**: The MacBook Air is a great choice for students and teachers because it is small, light, and works well with Apple's environment. The M4 chip makes this better by giving you enough power to do more than one thing at once and use programs like word processors, spreadsheets, presentation software, and research tools. It is a flexible tool for school projects because it supports creative apps like video editing and graphic design.
- o **Professionals and Business Users**: People who work as professionals and need a reliable laptop for work, managing projects, and internet meetings will like the MacBook Air with the M4 chip. Because it is designed to use little power, it can handle everyday tasks like email, changing documents, and videoconferencing without slowing down. The device is very portable, which makes it great for people who work while they're on the go. They can easily take it with them between meetings or on trips.
- o **Creative Professionals**: The M4 chip in the MacBook Air is powerful enough for light to moderate creative work, even though it's not as powerful as the M4 chip in the MacBook Pro. This includes making graphics, changing photos, making music, and sometimes even editing videos on a smaller scale. Professionals in the creative field who value portability and battery life will love the MacBook Air. It could even be used as a backup device for a more powerful desktop setup.
- o **Casual Users**: The MacBook Air with the M4 chip has more than enough power for people whose main uses for their computers are to browse the web, watch videos, use social media, and play light games. The M4 chip's efficiency means users can enjoy all-day battery life, making it great for use at home or on the go. Its fanless design makes it quiet to use.
- o **Developers and Coders**: The MacBook Pro is better for jobs that need a lot of power, like software development. However, the MacBook Air with the M4 chip can still work for developers who do less demanding coding tasks. Programming in languages like Python, JavaScript, and Swift is possible with it, as well as integrated development environments

(IDEs). This makes it perfect for web development, mobile app development, and even some game development.

Typical Use Cases

1. **Academic Work and Research**: The MacBook Air is used by teachers and students to take notes, write papers, do research, and make slideshows. It's easy to carry around campus because it's small and light, and the powerful M4 chip makes sure it works smoothly even when multiple programs are open at the same time.

2. **Business and Productivity Tasks**: The MacBook Air is used by professionals to do things like make reports, organize files, hold virtual meetings, and oversee projects. The performance of the M4 chip makes it possible to process data quickly, and the device's battery life means that it can be used all day without having to be charged.

3. **Making Content:** Creative people use the MacBook Air to edit photos, make digital art, and do some light video editing. The M4 chip has enough power to run programs like Adobe Photoshop, Final Cut Pro, and Logic Pro, which makes it a good choice for mobile video creators.

4. **Entertainment and Media Consumption**: Regular people like to watch movies, browse the web, and use social media on their MacBook Airs. You can enjoy watching movies, listening to music, or playing games in a great way with the high-quality Retina display and the fast M4 chip.

5. **Software Developers**: The MacBook Air is used to write and test code for web or mobile apps by software developers. The M4 chip can compile code and run simulators, which makes it a good choice for developers who want something portable without giving up too much speed.

To sum up, the MacBook Air with the M4 chip is great for a wide range of people, from students and teachers to pros and artists, because it is powerful, portable, and efficient. It's usually used for everything from schoolwork and productivity to making content and having fun for fun. This makes it a useful device for many situations.

CHAPTER 1
SETTING UP

This chapter is your starting point for mastering the fundamentals of this device. We will walk you through how to charge your device, initial set-up, basic navigations, battery levels, and all basic information you need to get started with your MacBook.

Locate the charging port on your Mac

There may be a MagSafe 3 port on your Mac as well as USB-C ports. Both ports can be used to charge your battery if your Mac has them.

- The MagSafe 3 port is near the escape key on the left side of the back of the computer.
- The computer has USB-C ports on the left side or both sides.

Charge with MagSafe 3

1. Connect the USB-C power charger to a wall outlet.
2. Connect the MagSafe 3 cable's USB-C end to the power charger.
3. Hook up the other end of the wire to your Mac's MagSafe 3 port.

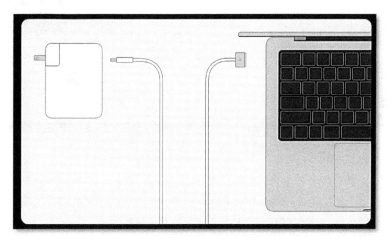

If your battery is fully charged, the light will glow green after you connect the charger. If your battery is charging, the light will glow amber.

If the indicator light flashes

If the indicator light on the MagSafe 3 connector flashes amber repeatedly, try these steps:

- Take the USB-C to MagSafe 3 Cable off of both your Mac and the power charger.
- Take the USB-C power charger out of the wall outlet.

- Clean the MagSafe 3 port with a dry cloth. Make sure there is nothing stuck in or on either the port or the connection.
- Make sure there is nothing in the USB-C port on the power charger or the USB-C connector.
- Start up your Mac again.
- When you're ready to charge, plug the USB-C power adapter into the wall and connect the USB-C to MagSafe 3 cable to both the adapter and your Mac.

Charge with USB-C

- Connect the power adapter to a wall port.
- Connect the power charger to one end of the USB-C cable.
- Connect the other end of the cord to your Mac's USB-C port.

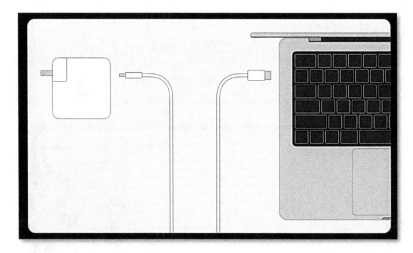

You can also connect a display that charges over USB-C or Thunderbolt, like the Apple Studio Display. You don't need to add a separate USB-C power adapter if your display gives your Mac power. When you connect more than one power charger to the USB-C ports and MagSafe 3 port (if it's there), your Mac will only charge through one port at a time. Make sure to choose the right USB-C charge cable because they handle various maximum wattages (W). If you plug in more than one power source, your Mac will only charge from the cable and power adapter or display that gives it the most power.

Checking the battery charger level

- Plug the power charger into the MacBook Air.
- Connect the power adapter to a wall port.

- Look at the menu bar in the top right corner of the screen. Ideally, an icon for the battery will show up.
- There will be a drop-down menu when you click the battery icon.
- The dropdown menu's display of the battery level is a percentage tag. This number shows how much charge is still in the battery.

If the battery is fully charged, the number will be 100%. There will be less of a percentage if it is only halfway paid. A lightning bolt sign can also be seen in the battery icon if the MacBook Air is currently charging. Furthermore, you can get more detailed information about the battery state by choosing "**Battery Preferences" or "Energy Saver Preferences**" from the dropdown menu. This will open the Battery options pane in System Settings. Here you can see more information about the battery's health, settings, and power use.

Save Battery

To optimize battery performance and extend the lifespan of your Mac, follow these steps:

1. **Open System Settings:**

   - Click on the **Apple menu** ( ) at the top-left corner of your screen.
   - Select **System Settings** from the drop-down menu.

2. **Access Battery Settings:**

   - In the System Settings window, find and select **Battery** from the sidebar. You might need to scroll down to locate this option.

3. **Adjust Battery Preferences:**

   - **Low Power Mode:** To manage power usage, choose from the options next to **Low Power Mode**:
     - Select **"Always"** to have Low Power Mode enabled at all times.
     - Choose **"Only on battery"** to enable it only when running on battery power.
     - Opt for **"Only on power adapter"** to activate Low Power Mode when connected to a power source.

   - **Battery Health:** Click the **Info button** next to **Battery Health** to access additional settings. Ensure that **Optimized Battery Charging** is enabled to enhance battery health over time. You may also enable **"Manage battery longevity"** to further extend the life of your battery.
   - **Options for Sleep and Graphics:** Click **Options** on the right side to adjust additional settings:

- Enable **"Put hard disks to sleep when possible"** to save power by allowing the hard disks to enter sleep mode during inactivity.
- Turn on **"Automatic graphics switching"** to switch between integrated and discrete graphics as needed, reducing power consumption when high graphics performance is not required.

Charging Habits That Will Prolong Your MacBook's Battery Life

As long as you buy a new MacBook, the battery life will be what it says it will be. But over time, your MacBook's battery life will slowly but surely get worse. Lithium-ion batteries, which are used in MacBooks, smartphones, and most other tools, naturally lose power over time. So, there's no way to make sure that the battery in your MacBook is always healthy. But you can make the battery life of your MacBook last longer by charging it the right way. Here, we talk about the best ways to charge your MacBook so that the battery lasts longer.

1. Don't Fully Charge or Drain Your Battery

As we already said, MacBooks use lithium-ion batteries, which lose some of their power as you charge and discharge them. The battery's highest charging capacity goes down a little with each full charge cycle. Lithium-ion batteries lose a lot of power when they are fully charged because they can leak electricity and shorten their life. This is why you may have noticed that the battery in your MacBook charges more quickly from 0% to 80% and then more slowly from 80% to 100%. On the other hand, fully draining lithium-ion batteries is just as bad. For the best battery life, Battery University says to keep your charge between 30% and 80%. But it's hard to keep your battery from dying completely, so if you ever need to work somewhere without an outlet, we suggest getting one of the best laptop power banks.

2. Use Apple's Official Charger

Even though it may seem obvious, it's always good to point this out. Apple always gives you a power charger and a USB-C charging cable when you buy a new MacBook. It is always best to use an official power adapter and charging cord because they are designed to keep your battery healthy over time.

It's not just about how long the batteries last either. It's also safer to use a charger made by Apple for a MacBook. But it's important to note that you can use some great chargers for MacBooks that aren't made by Apple. Just stay away from cheap third-party MacBook chargers from unknown brands, as they can be dangerous and detrimental to the battery's long-term health. Apple chargers are the best ones to buy if you're going to buy one. If not, get one from a reliable company like Anker, Satechi, or Belkin. You can use Apple's website to determine which third-party chargers are the best because it even sells select devices from outside vendors.

3. Enable Optimized Battery Charging

Your MacBook has a feature called "**Optimized Battery Charging**" that learns how you usually charge it and changes how it charges to help the battery last longer. This function is meant to keep your battery in better shape. It does this by waiting to charge your battery past 80% if it thinks you will be leaving your MacBook plugged in for a long time. When you take the charger out of the wall, this function makes sure that the battery is fully charged. In macOS' **System Settings**, you can enable Optimized Battery Charging. Select **Battery** from the left side, and then click the "**Info" (i)** button next to "**Battery Health**" and turn on "**optimized battery charging.**"

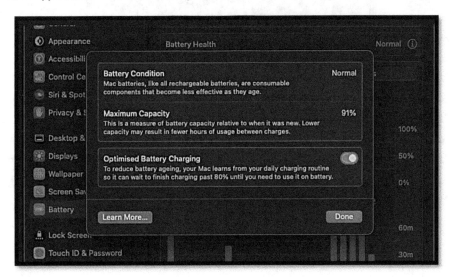

As we already said, it's best to keep your power level between 30% and 80%. Optimized Battery Charging does not stop your battery from charging past 80%, though. Keeping tabs on your battery level while you concentrate on your work can be distracting, and it only slows the process. Another thing you can do to keep your battery from charging past 80% is to use the app AlDente. This app stops your Mac's battery from charging past a certain number even when it's plugged in. It works with macOS 11 Big Sur and later, and you can get it for free. You can also pay for a version with more features.

4. Don't Leave Your MacBook Constantly Plugged In

A lot of people work with their MacBooks plugged in all the time. We all do it, but MacBooks aren't meant to be plugged in all the time. As we already said, charging your battery to 100% could make it warm, which would shorten the life of your MacBook's battery in the long run. Because of this, you shouldn't always have your MacBook plugged in.

5. Half-Charge Your MacBook for Long-Term Storage

You need to control the temperature and battery rate of your MacBook if you want to put it away for a while. These two things will shorten the life of your MacBook's battery while it's being stored. Apple says that if you need to store your MacBook for a long time, you should charge the battery to about 50%.

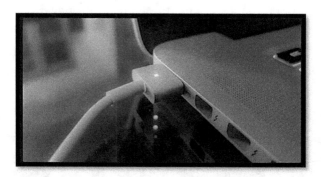

The recommended amount is 50% because if you fully charge your battery and then store it for a long time, it may lose some of its power, which will shorten its life. Apple says that if you leave it fully discharged for a long time, "the battery could fall into a deep discharge state, which makes it incapable of holding a charge." On top of that, Apple says that you should store your device somewhere cooler than 90 degrees F and charge it to 50% every six months if you plan to keep it for longer than that. Also, if you don't plan to use your Mac for a long time, you should turn it off.

6. Charge Your MacBook at Moderate Ambient Temperatures

Any kind of battery will die if it gets too hot. The Battery University says that because charging lithium-ion batteries is so delicate, it needs to be done with great care. Apple also says that charging your device in hot conditions can lower the battery's power. The company says that the ideal temperature range is 50 to 95 degrees F. If your MacBook case gets hot while it's charging, you might want to take it off first.

Getting Ready

1. **Power On Your Mac:**
    - Tap the **Power button** to turn on your Mac. The setup process will start.
2. **Choose a Language:**
    - Select your preferred language from the list. This choice will determine the language used throughout the system for all text and communication.

- o After selecting, click **Continue** to proceed.

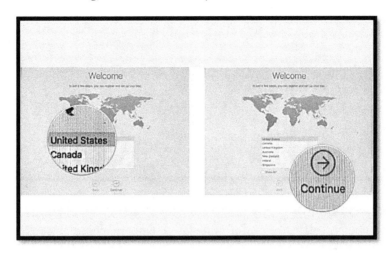

3. **Pick a Keyboard Layout:**
   - o Pick a keyboard layout that matches your preference. The layout you select will dictate how your keystrokes are interpreted by the system, regardless of the physical appearance of the keyboard.
   - o Once chosen, tap **Continue** to move forward.

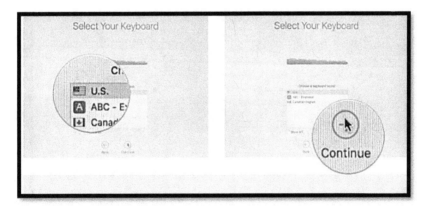

4. **Connect to a Wi-Fi Network:**
   - o If you're using Wi-Fi, select your network from the list.
   - o If you are connecting via Ethernet, select **Other Network Options** and choose **Ethernet**.
   - o Enter your Wi-Fi password if necessary and tap **Continue**. The system may take some time to connect, and you might see a spinning wheel with the message **"Looking for networks."**

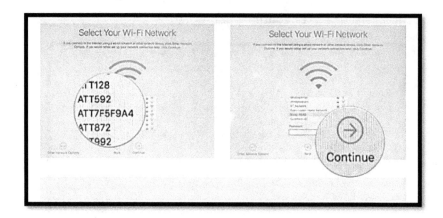

5. **Decide on Data Transfer:**
   - If you're setting up your Mac as a new machine, pick **don't transfer any information now**.
   - If you're migrating from another Mac, follow the provided guidelines for transferring your data.
   - If you're switching from a PC, select the appropriate option and follow the instructions.
   - Click **Continue** after making your selection.

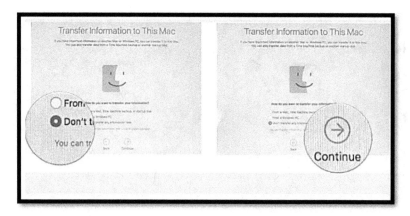

6. **Enable or Disable Location Services:**
   - Check the box next to **Enable Location Services** if you want to allow features like Siri, Maps, and Spotlight recommendations to access your location.
   - If you prefer not to share your location with Apple, leave this option unchecked.
   - Tap **Continue** to proceed.

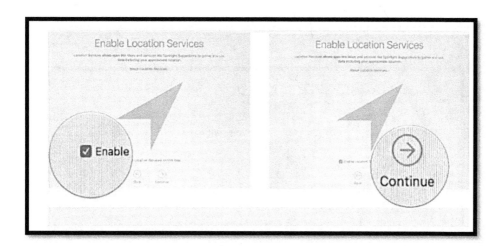

7. **Sign In with Your Apple ID:**
   - Log in using your Apple ID to sync services across all your Apple devices, such as iPhone, iPad, Apple TV, and other Macs.
   - If you don't have an Apple ID or prefer to create one later, you can skip this step and sign in later from your Mac or through your iPhone or iPad.
   - If you have two-factor authentication enabled, you will need to verify your identity.
   - After signing in or skipping, tap **Continue**.

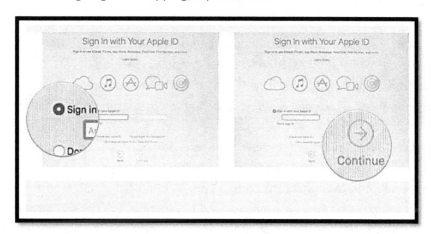

8. **Set Up Your Account:**
   - Provide a full name for your computer. If you log in with your Apple ID, this field may automatically populate.
   - Next, assign a name to your user account, which may also auto-fill if you used your Apple ID.

- o Once you have entered these details, click **Continue** to finalize your account setup.

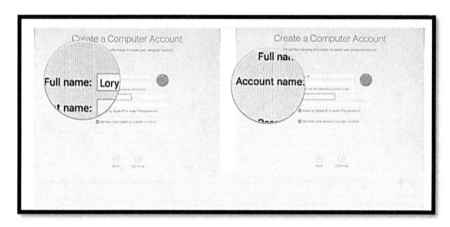

These steps will guide you through the initial setup of your Mac, allowing you to configure it according to your preferences and requirements. Once complete, your Mac will be ready for use.

Transfer information from another computer

You can move all of your files, emails, accounts, and other information from a Windows computer to a new Mac. If you want to move from a different Mac you own. Your options for connecting your Windows PC to your MacBook Air are either wireless data transmission or an Ethernet connection.

Before you begin: Make sure that your windows computer has the most current version of all of its software. Then, get Migration Assistant on your Windows machine.

Wireless data transfer is possible. Your new Mac and Windows computer needs to be linked to the same Wi-Fi network. Click your Windows machine on the setup screen and then do what it says.

Move files around with an Ethernet cable. One way to connect your Mac to your Windows computer is with an Ethernet wire. You'll need an Ethernet adapter, like the Belkin USB-C to Gigabit Ethernet Adapter, to connect the cord to your MacBook Air's USB-C port. If your Ethernet cable doesn't have enough ports, you might need an adaptor to connect it to your Windows machine. After they are linked, click on your windows computer to see the setup page and then follow the on-screen instructions. After that, send data. You can also choose not to send any info at this time. In that case, choose Not Now in the Migration Assistant Window.

Establish your computer account and log in using your Apple ID.

Use your Apple ID to log in. If you have an iPad, iPhone, or other Apple object, you probably already have one. If not, you can make one right now for free. An email address and a password make up your Apple ID. You use it for everything on Apple, like getting into iCloud, the Apple TV app, the App Store, and more. Your Apple ID is different from the username and password you use to log in to your Mac account. It's best to keep your Apple ID secret and not share it with anyone.

On this screen, do any of the following:

- If you have an Apple ID, your iPhone or iPad will show you a proof code. Type in your email address and password to get to your Apple ID. If you don't have an iPhone or iPad, a proof code is sent to the phone number that's linked to your Apple ID. If you don't get the SMS or proof code, follow the steps shown on the screen.
- Click "**Create new Apple ID**" if you don't have one already.
- Choose "**Forgot Apple ID or password**" if you can't remember your Apple ID or password.
- If you don't want to make an Apple ID or sign in with one right now, click Set up Later. Choose "**Sign in with your Apple ID**" from the menu of System Settings once everything has been set up. From there, you can either use a current Apple ID to sign in or make a new one.

After you log in with your Apple ID, read the terms and conditions. If you agree, check the box and click agree to move on.

Create a computer account: After adding your name, make up a name for the account and a password. This will let you get into your MacBook Air and let other things happen. You can give an extra hint to help you remember your computer account password if you can't remember it. Choose a different picture to use as your login picture by clicking it. However, if you check this box during setup, you can use your Apple ID to change the password to get into your Mac if you forget it. It's not the same as your Apple ID or bank account.

Use this as your new Mac

If you have already set up a device running iOS 15 or later or iPadOS 15 or later, a screen that says "**Make This Your New Mac**" will display. This option speeds up the setup process. If your iPad or iPhone doesn't have the latest software, you won't be able to see this step. When setting up Make This Your New Mac, use the settings from your iCloud account to skip a lot of setup steps tag. To use the settings you already have, click **Continue**. The setup process will then move on to setting up Apple Pay and Touch ID. If you want to change a setting on your brand-new MacBook Air, click **Customize Settings** and proceed to the next step. Change your Mac's private and security settings, turn on Screen Time, and make Siri available.

Turn on Location Services: Open **System Settings**, click **Privacy & Security** in the sidebar, then click Location Services and choose your options. To change your Location Services settings later, turn them on. Turn on Location Services. To use your Mac's location, choose whether to enable applications like Maps. Should you choose not to use Location Services, you will see a screen where you can pick your time zone.

Share analytics with Apple and Developers. Navigate to **System Settings**, select Privacy & Security from the sidebar, then click Analytics & Improvements (you may have to scroll down), and finally choose your options. You can choose whether to send data and reports to Apple and whether Apple can share usage and crash data with developers.

Set up Screen Time. You can keep track of how much time you spend on your MacBook Air every day and week with Screen Time. You can also limit your kids' screen time and tell them how long they can use certain apps. To turn it off, click Set up Later. To turn it on, click Continue. Enter System Settings and select Screen Time from the sidebar to choose your options if you decide to set them up later.

Use FileVault to protect your files. FileVault is one way to help keep your info safe. In addition to enabling FileVault to protect your data during setup, you can also enable your iCloud account to open your disk if you forget your password.

Turn on Siri and say, "Hey Siri." You can turn on Siri and "Hey Siri" during setup, which lets you tell Siri what to do. For Siri to work, click "Enable Ask Siri." When Siri asks you to set up "Hey Siri," say a few commands. Then, go to System Settings, select Siri & Spotlight from the sidebar, and make your choices to turn on Siri and say "Hello Siri" later. You might also choose to share sounds with Apple to make Siri better while you're setting it up. In the end, you can always choose not to share the audio. In the menu of System Settings, go to **Privacy & Security**. Then, choose **Analytics & Improvements** (you may have to scroll down).

Accessories you'll need

When setting up your MacBook Air 2025, there are a few tools that might help you get more done, stay connected, and keep your work safe. Here are some more things to think about:

- The MacBook Air 2025 has USB-C connectors, so a **USB-C hub or dock** might give you more ways to join. Pick one that has extra USB-A ports, Wi-Fi, SD card slots, HDMI or DisplayPort output, and extra USB-A ports.
- Although the MacBook Air comes with built-in storage, you may want to buy **solid-state drives (SSDs) or portable hard drives** to add to your storage space or make a copy of your important files.
- The use of a **USB-C to USB-A converter** will enable you to use older USB-A accessories and devices with your MacBook Air.
- If you need a bigger screen or want to set up two displays side by side, you might want to buy an **external monitor** with a USB-C or Thunderbolt 3 connection.

- Even though the MacBook Air has a trackpad built in, some users find it more comfortable and accurate to use an **extra mouse or trackpad**. Trackpad or mouse with Bluetooth. Pick out a Bluetooth mouse or touchscreen that works for you.
- **Laptop Stand**: With the help of a laptop stand, you can raise your MacBook Air to a more comfortable viewing height and improve airflow to keep it cool. This can help your neck, and arms feel less stressed after using it for a long time.
- You might want to use a **keyboard cover or skin** to protect your MacBook Air's keyboard from spills, dirt, and scratches. They come in many styles and materials so you can find one that you like.
- **Case or Sleeve for Laptop**: A case or sleeve for your laptop keeps it safe when you're on the go. Pick one that is padded, made of strong materials, and fits close to the foot.
- Even though the MacBook Air comes with a power adapter, it might be helpful to have a second **USB-C power adapter**, especially if you move or work in a lot of different places.
- To make or receive secret video calls, you need a pair of **headphones or earbuds**. Pick the ones that are comfortable and have good sound.
- If you want to protect your privacy, you can put a webcam cover over the built-in camera on the MacBook Air when it's not in use.
- The microfiber wipes, screen cleaner, and keyboard cleaner in a cleaning kit can help get rid of dust, fingerprints, and smudges on your MacBook Air so it looks and works its best.

These are some of the things that come with the MacBook Air that might make you happier with it. Depending on your needs and preferences, you could also gain from different accessories.

Exploring the macOS Desktop and Interface

There are many parts to the macOS interface that make it easy and stable for users to work with the OS and their programs. Some of them are the menu bar, managing files, going full screen, dock panels, and other parts. Down at the bottom of the screen is the Dock. Up at the top is the menu bar. Your desk is where you work.

Desktop

The Desktop is where you do your work.

The desktop experience on the MacBook Air 2025 is about the same as on other Macs that run macOS. At the bottom of the screen is a dock that has quick links to the apps you use most often. You can also make the dock your own by adding and removing apps from it. As the background for your desktop, you can use a picture you've made yourself or one of the many photos that come with macOS. On top of that, you can add widgets to your screen to show information like news, the weather, and more.

Menu Bar

You can find the menu bar at the very top of your macOS screen. You can use your Mac and work with many programs because it gives you access to many system and application menus.

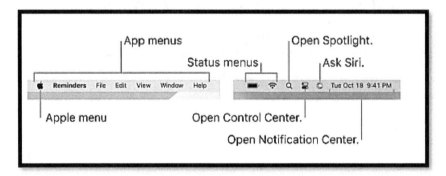

What is on the Mac menu bar?

Here are some of the most important things that you can usually find on the menu bar.

- o **Apple Menu**: Users can get to system-level functions and settings through the Apple menu, which is on the left side of the menu bar and is represented by the Apple logo.

From this spot, you can get to System Settings, software updates, sleep, restart, and stop, among other things.

- ○ **Application Menus**: The menus on the right side of the menu bar change depending on the app that is currently open. You can find options and directions that are specific to the program you are using in these menus. They are usually next to the Apple menu and show the name of the app that is currently running.
- ○ **System Icons**: The system icons are on the right side of the menu bar and make it easy to get to important features and settings. Some of the symbols that can be used are Wi-Fi, Bluetooth, battery life, noise control, the date, and the time.
- ○ **Spotligh**t: On the right side of the menu bar, you can see an icon that looks like a magnifying glass. It can be clicked to open Spotlight, a search tool that works across the whole system. You can use Spotlight to find files, start programs, do math, get definitions, and more.
- ○ **Notifications**: You can find the Notification Center icon on the right side, next to the Spotlight button. There look to be three stacked lines. When you click on this icon, the Notification Center opens. From there, you can see and handle alerts from different programs.

How to change the time zone manually

No matter where you are, your Mac will change your time zone immediately. You can select a time zone, though. If you choose a different time zone in the system settings, your Mac will change the clock to match the new location.

The following are the steps:

- ○ Select "**System Settings**" from the Apple menu.
- ○ Choose "**Time Zone**" in the "**Date and Time**" section.
- ○ By deselecting "**Set Time Zone Automatically Using Current Location**" and using the map, you can set the time zone by hand.
- ○ The "**Closest City**" setting can also be used to choose your city. You can choose a place on your Mac, and the time and date will just appear.

The Finder

Finder is macOS's built-in graphical user interface and file management system. It gives users a central place to find their files and control their applications. The main Finder menu bar is a fixed feature that sits at the top of your screen and gives you access to different Mac settings and functions. Opening new windows and changing the view options are both controlled by this menu bar. The Finder app is the main tool for handling files on a Mac. It works like Windows Explorer. The interface is simple and easy to use. The left-hand panel is usually used to display the directory of files and shortcuts. This area makes it easy to get to places you use often, like your desktop, documents, downloads, and any drives that are linked. The chosen directory's contents will show up on the right, letting you look through your saved files, programs, and other things. Finder lets you access and work with all of your Mac's files. You can not only see your files and put them in order, but you can also make new folders, copy things, and get rid of files you don't want right from the interface. Additionally, Finder's search feature is very strong, making it easy to find specific files or go to specific directories. Finder will display results from all of your Mac's storage, including metadata and content inside files, as soon as you type your search query into the search bar. With the release of macOS Mojave, Finder got a visual and practical makeover that made it even easier to use. The ability to preview files right in the Finder window is one of the most noticeable features. This preview pane on the side lets you quickly look at pictures, movies, documents, and other things without having to open them in their programs. You can find and handle your files faster and better with this feature because it streamlines the browsing process. Overall, Finder is an important part of macOS because it provides a strong and easy-to-use way to handle files and move between them. The fact that it works with the system and has strong search and preview tools makes it an essential and flexible part of the Mac experience.

Control Center

The Control Center on your Mac lets you know when your camera, microphone, or location is being used and gives you quick access to settings like Airdrop, Wi-Fi, and Focus. To make Control Center more unique, you can add things like details about the battery life, quick user switching, or accessibility shortcuts.

1. On your Mac, go to the menu bar and click on **Control Center** .
2. Pick one of these **Control Center** things to use:
   - You can change a setting by moving a slider. For example, to change how loud your Mac is, drag the Sound slider.
   - Toggle a function on or off by clicking the symbol for it, such as Airdrop or Bluetooth.
   - To view more options, click on an item or the arrow next to it. Click Focus to display a list of your Focuses and turn any of them on or off or click Screen Mirroring to select a target display.

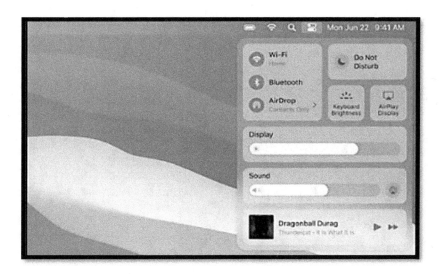

Notification Center

There is a useful tool in macOS called the "**Mac Notification Center**" that lets you see notifications from all of your installed apps simultaneously. This feature gives you a quick look at alerts and changes that might need your attention but don't need an answer right away. Instead of getting in the way, the Notification Center lets you read these alerts whenever you want. This way, you can keep working and not miss any important information. The Mac Notification Center's customization options are one of its main advantages. Customers can choose which app notifications to see in the Notification Center and how to display them. With this much control, you'll only see the messages that are important to you. This will help you stay focused and keep your workspace clean. You can choose to get banners, which are short-term alerts that show up in the upper right corner of your screen, or alerts, which you have to interact with before they go away. You can easily change your settings if there are some apps whose notifications you don't want or that bother you. You can directly hide certain apps from showing up in the Notification Center, so they don't take up too much space in your notification feed. This is especially helpful for apps that send you a lot of low-priority messages that you might not need to see right away.

Launch the notification center

For each app that you can't handle quickly, the Mac Notification Center will stack alerts and messages for that app. In this case, if Google Chrome sends you a lot of alerts, they will all be put together into one note. To see all the alerts in a stack, all you have to do is select the top notification. To get rid of all alerts related to a specific app, hover over the X button and choose Clear All.

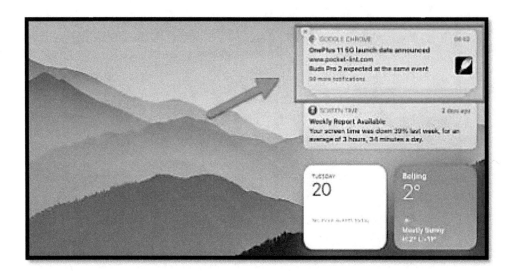

How to erase notifications

In the upper right area of your screen is an icon that looks like three lines stacked on top of each other. If you click on this icon, you can delete all alerts on your MacBook Air 2023. After that, scroll up to see all of your warnings. Once you click the "**X**" button next to each warning, you can delete it. Move your mouse over a message and then hold it over the "X" button to get rid of all the notifications for that app. The "**Clear All**" button will show up. Click it. By going to **System Settings > Notification**, choosing the app or website on the right, and then unchecking "**Allow notifications**," you can turn off alerts for certain apps and websites on your MacBook Air 2025.

Updating macOS

On your MacBook Air 2023, you can use Software Update to get changes and improvements for macOS and its built-in programs, like Safari. This is how it works:

- Click on the **Apple sign** in the upper left corner of your screen to bring up the Apple menu. Then, choose System Settings. Select "System Settings" from the drop-down menu that shows how to access your Mac's preferences and other settings.
- Select **General** from the left. If you need to, scroll down and click on "**General**." This area has some basic settings that affect how your Mac works in general.
- Click **Software Update** on the right. The "**Software Update**" option is on the right side of the window when you're in the "General" space. This will make your Mac check for any available changes to the macOS system when you click it.
- If an update is available, click "**Update Now**." If your Mac finds a new update, you'll see the "**Update Now**" button. Click this to start the download process. To finish the update,

your Mac might need to restart, so make sure you've saved any work before you go ahead with it.

If there are any updates available, they will be listed next to the App Store. If you go to the Apple menu, you can also update apps you got from the App Store. Select App Store to continue using the app.

Using the Trackpad

Apple has come up with 15 known finger movements that you can use on a multi-touch keyboard to get things done. You probably already know at least a few of them by heart, but you might not have had a chance to learn others that could help you over time. If you can remember these 10 movements, you'll be able to use your trackpad more quickly and comfortably. Using motions has an extra benefit besides saving time, even if it takes a moment to remember them all. The number of times an annoying and time-wasting gesture is used by mistake on the trackpad should also go down.

1. **Tap to click**

It makes sense to start teaching someone how to use a keyboard by showing them how to click with one finger. The user can select a section of a document in a word processor by using this most basic gesture, which also lets them click on linked text and images on websites. You're not going anywhere without it. When you double-tap, you can start a file, folder, or app, which is probably the most common action.

2. **Secondary click (right click)**

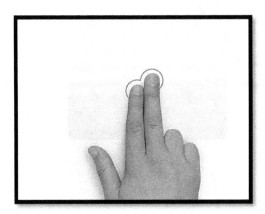

Since you already have the first two important ones, these next moves will only make your weapons stronger. To right-click, you don't have to press Control and tap with one finger. You can click or tap with two fingers instead. This click can help your curlicue, which is the part of your hand between your thumb and fingers, feel better.

3. **Scroll**

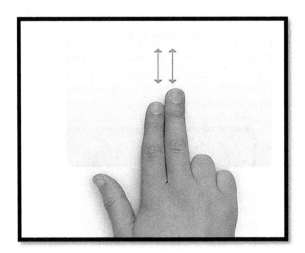

People who use a trackpad know and use this next key motion as often as they breathe: slide two fingers up or down (usually the forefinger and middle finger) to scroll through websites and documents. On websites, word processing pages, and Finder windows, the slider bar on the right edge is still useful for quickly skipping through a lot of pages. But this motion will be better for getting to the specifics.

4. Drag with three fingers

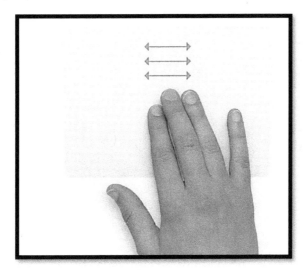

Three-finger drag is different from the other movements in that you need to go to Accessibility preferences in System Settings to make it work. If you want to drag and drop things on your screen in a way that is better for your body than using your thumb and pointer, you can use three fingers and then tap or click.

5. Zoom in or out

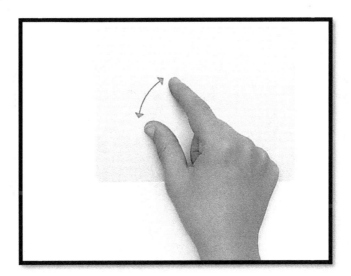

You need to use two fingers to pinch and zoom in or stretch and zoom out of words or icons. But be careful not to zoom out too far and see all of your tabs split up into small windows. Depending on how you usually use tabs, that could be jarring.

6. Smart zoom

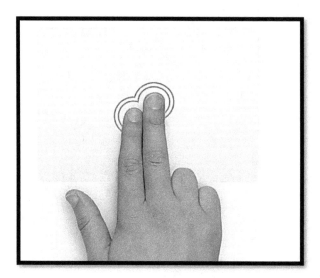

Smart zoom is another two-finger motion that can help you see better. With two taps, you can quickly zoom in and out of a page or picture. This is not the same as the zoom-in or out motion because you can only zoom in or out one level.

7. **Rotate**

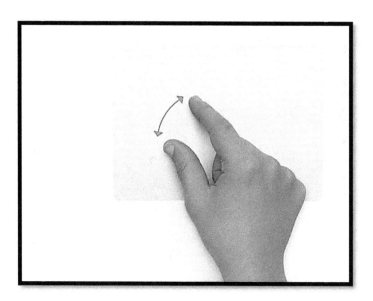

When we talk about pictures, you can also spin them by moving two fingers around each other. With this, you can change the direction of the image if you think it would be more interesting that way. It may take some practice to be able to do turn in small steps.

8. **Mission Control**

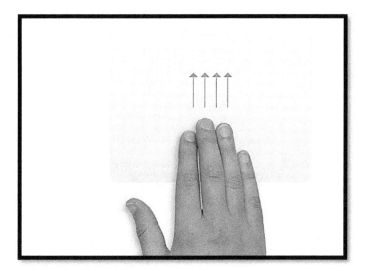

When you want to see a list of all the apps and windows that are open, you can swipe up with four fingers to get to Mission Control.

9. **Launchpad**

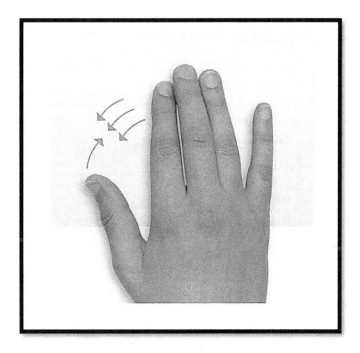

Launchpad lets you look through your apps visually. To get to it, pinch your thumb and three fingers together. It helps a lot when you need to get rid of some to make room for new ones.

10. **Show desktop**

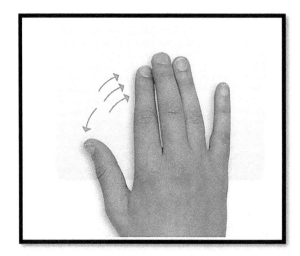

To see the desktop, move your thumb and three fingers apart. If you don't check it every so often, it can quickly become cluttered and distracting. This motion and the opposite one on the Launchpad can both help you keep your Mac's user interface clean.

How to Change MacBook Sleep Settings

Putting MacBook to sleep manually

You can manually hibernate your MacBook in one of the following ways:

- Go to the Apple menu and choose "Sleep".

- Press the power button and then the sleep button.
- Close the lid and the notebook will enter sleep mode by default.

If your MacBook has an IR port, you can use Apple Remote to change the time to sleep, put it into hibernation mode, or wake it up from sleep:

- To go to sleep mode, press and hold the Play/Pause button for 5 seconds.
- To turn on your MacBook, press any button on the remote.

How to change MacBook sleep time setting

You can set your MacBook to sleep after a certain amount of time, like one minute to three hours of not being used. You can also stop your device from going to sleep.

To change the settings for your MacBook's sleep, first tap the Apple icon in the upper left area of the screen, then select "System **Settings** " and then "Battery." In this area, you can find the power settings.

On the Battery tab:

- Set the time gap for the "**Turn off display after**" slider. The screen will go into sleep mode after that time.
- Enable the laptop to wake up from sleep mode and check for new emails by turning on Power Nap while using battery power.

You can do the following on the Power Adapter tab:

- To select the amount of time to wait before turning off automatically, move the "Turn off display after" slider.
- Stop the device from immediately entering hibernation mode when the display is off.
- Let the device wake up from sleep mode when Wi-Fi is turned on or when an app asks to connect to the network.
- Let you get out of sleep mode to do things like check email or messengers.

How to adjust a MacBook sleep timer

If you have a set plan and know exactly when you won't be using your Mac, you can set it to hibernate. For instance, you go to sleep around midnight and forget to turn off your device a lot of the time. **Set your MacBook to hibernate at midnight, and it won't turn on until morning, which will drain the battery:**

- Click on "**System Settings**" under "Apple" in the upper left part of the screen.
- Select "Schedule" from the battery settings menu.
- Pick the day of the week and time you want your Mac to go to sleep, then click **OK**.

Enter "**Terminal**" from "**Applications**" and "**Utilities**" to put your device to sleep. To turn off the device, type sudo shutdown, press the space bar, and type -h. To restart, type -r, and to suspend, type -s. After the space bar, type + and then the number of minutes you want to use. Then press "**Return**."

How to Optimize Your Mac with Power Management Settings

Managing power well is very important for a Mac, especially since one of the best things about Apple laptops is that they have batteries that last all day (up to 10 hours). Managing power well is needed to do that, though, and if you've ever looked at the Energy Saver settings in the **System Settings** app, you know that they don't let you use all of your Mac's features. Yes, you can change some important settings using the well-designed graphical user interface. But if you want to understand how these settings affect your Mac's general performance, you will need to know a few tricks. That's where we come in...

Default power management settings coming with your Mac

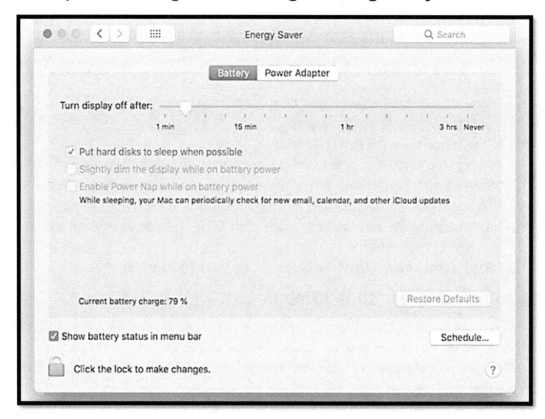

By choosing About **This Mac > System Information > Power > System Power Settings**, you can access the power management settings that are already set up on every Mac by clicking the Apple icon. This is where the settings for both AC and battery power control are. This section explains how long a time of inactivity it will take before the display goes to sleep (this can be changed in the Energy Saver screen), or the system goes into standby (if this feature is enabled). The type of hibernation that is allowed on the Mac is also described here.

How the Mac goes into Safe Sleep depends on the type of sleep mode it is in. You may already know that when you leave your computer alone for a while, it goes into different energy-saving modes. These include rest mode, hibernate mode, safe sleep mode, and sleep mode.

How to customize the Mac's power management settings

The average user won't start messing around with these settings, but if you know what they do, you can improve your Mac's performance by changing the power management settings. You may remember that sometimes waking up on the computer takes longer than normal. If you want to speed up your Mac, changing the power management settings for it hibernate mode is a good place to start. **The steps are the same as the ones we showed you for sleep mode, but this time the goal is hibernate mode.**

1. Launch Terminal and type:pmset -g |grep hibernatemode

2. This will trigger a response **detailing the current setting of the Mac**. It should be either 0, 3, or 25. The answer should look something like this: hibernatemode 3

```
●  ●  ●                    ⌂ ▬▬ — -bash — 70×9
Last login: Thu Apr  5 16:12:46 on ttys000
[▬▬▬-MacBook-Pro:~ ▬▬$ pmset -g |grep hibernatemode              ]
  hibernatemode          3
 ▬▬▬-MacBook-Pro:~ ▬▬$ ▮
```

Understanding the different hibernate mode settings

When you turn on a desktop Mac, it goes into **hibernate mode 0**. This means that the system won't write the contents of the RAM to the disk, so if the power goes out, you lose your data. When you turn on a portable Mac, it will automatically go into **hibernate mode 3**. This mode stores a copy of the memory on the internal disk and keeps the memory powered while the computer is shut down. If the power goes out, the Mac will still wake from memory unless it has to recover from a disk image. The "**pmset**" command in Terminal can only be used by the computer user to set **Hibernate mode 25**. It will write the data from the RAM to the SSD disk and turn off when you switch to **mode 25**. This changes how well the sleep-to-wake feature works overall (it will wake up more slowly), but it does help the battery last longer. Pick the setting that works best for your process right now. That is, if your Mac's hibernate mode was set to 0, you can change it to 3 by typing the following into Terminal: **pmset hibernatemode 3.**

CHAPTER 2

CUSTOMIZING YOUR MACBOOK M4

In this chapter, we will look at how to customize your MacBook to increase your productivity, comfort and meet your individual specification. We will look at how to find wallpaper for your MacBook, configuring the dock, control center, iCloud, external displays, and others.

Find a New Wallpaper for Your MacBook

Changing the default wallpaper is a good way to start customizing your Mac desktop, but it's not the most exciting way to do it. Apple comes with a bunch of wallpapers. You can also get it online. Downloading wallpaper is easy, and it only takes seconds to turn it on.

- Select Change Wallpaper from the drop-down menu when you right-click on your desktop.
- The Wallpaper tab will appear in the System Settings. Choose a desktop background (including dynamic wallpapers) or select a custom image from this point on.
- Click on **Add Photo > Choose** to choose your picture.

- Find the folder where you saved your new wallpaper picture, then select it and click "**Choose**" to make it your desktop background.

Customize the Control Center

Some parts of the Control Center can be changed to make your Mac even more unique. To get to all the customization choices, go to **System Settings > Control Center**. There will be a list of all the features in the Control Center in the box. These will include Wi-Fi, Bluetooth, AirDrop, Focus Mode, and more. Select the drop-down menu for each section as you go through the list. You can pick from three choices: **Always Show in Menu Bar, Show When Active, and Don't Show in Menu Bar**. Do this again for each section until everything is set up the way you want it.

Add Widgets to Your Mac Desktop

This feature in macOS should be known to people who use widgets on their iPhone home screens. The date is in the upper right area of the desktop. To get to your widgets and change them, click on it and then press **Edit Widgets** at the bottom of the screen.

After you do this, all of your Mac's tools will show up on a gray screen. You can look through widgets by topic or use the search bar to find specific ones. Click on the tool you want to add to your desktop when you find it. You can change the widget display by dragging the widgets around the screen after you have added all of the widgets you want. You can get rid of widgets by hitting the minus sign (−) in their upper right corner.

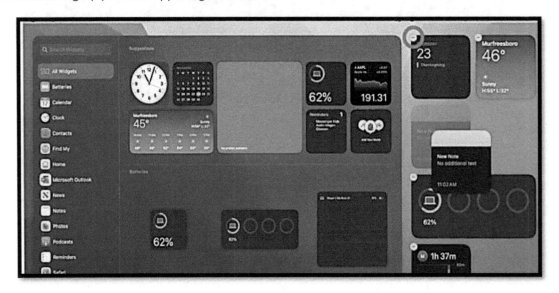

Personalize the Dock

The macOS Dock makes it easy to get to frequently used programs, pick up where you left off on open work, or keep browsing the Web. You can change the settings for your Dock if the ones that come with it don't work well for you.

Go to **System Settings > Desktop & Dock** to change how your Dock looks. **You can change any of the following choices from here:**

- **Size**: The slider bar lets you change the size of the Dock to suit your needs.
- **Magnification**: Move your mouse over the Dock and use the slider bar to change how big the icons are.
- **Position:** The drop-down menu lets you choose where on the desktop you want your Dock to be (bottom, left, or right).
- **Minimize Windows Using:** Choose between the Genie Effect and the Scale Effect when you close windows.
- **Double-Click**: Use the drop-down menu to choose whether clicking twice on the title bar of a window will make it zoom in, shrink, or do nothing.
- **Minimize Windows into Application Icon**: You can choose to have Windows reduced into the Dock icon for the application or as separate windows.
- **"Hide & Show"** lets you choose whether the Dock should always be shown or hidden by default.
- **Animate**: This is a toggle that lets you add movements (like bouncing) to the Dock when you open an app.
- **Indicators**: Slide this switch to show dots (indicators) below open apps in the Dock.
- **Suggested & Recent Apps**: Toggle this option to show recently used and frequently opened apps in the Dock.

Change Your Mac's Login Screen

You can change the image presented on your Mac's login window thanks to more recent macOS updates. Your Apple ID and contact card will both display the picture you choose. After going to **System Settings** and clicking on **Users and Groups**, you can change this. Next to your display name, there is a picture.

Choose between a Memoji, an Emoji, and a Monogram when the selection box appears. You can also use your Mac's camera or an image from the Photos app to take a picture.

Choose a New Style for Your Mac Icons

Adding your style to your Mac desktop is more than just picking out a wallpaper. In a few easy steps, you can also change the way desktop icons and files look. To change the icon for a file or folder on your desktop, copy the new picture to your clipboard, select the item you want to change, and then choose File > Get Info. First, click on the small button in the upper left corner of the information window. Then, go to the menu bar and choose **Edit > Paste**.

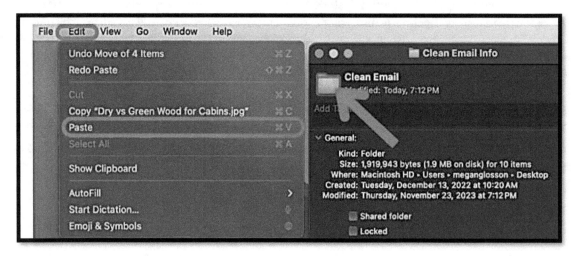

If a generic JPEG or PNG logo appears instead of the picture you chose, make sure you copied the image properly (the contents, not the file) and then pasted it. To change icons for **applications**, copy the image to your clipboard, then go to **Finder -> New Finder Window**, and choose **Applications**. Choose **File -> Get** Info after selecting the program. First, click on the small button in the upper left corner of the information window. Then, go to the menu bar and choose **Edit > Paste**. Keep in mind that some programs will need you to let Finder make these changes. To make this change, you must either use your fingerprint or enter your password.

Pick a Custom Color Scheme

Apple lets users mix and match different color schemes with the release of macOS Mojave. This gives you full control over the accent colors on your Mac desktop and lets you make it look the way you want it to. Apple has added more ways to change colors in newer versions of macOS, such as Dark Mode, Cursor colors, and changing the backgrounds in Finder. Go to **System Settings > Appearance** to change any of these things. Then, depending on the color changes you want to make, follow the extra steps in each part.

Light or Dark Mode

You can choose between Light, Dark, and Auto Mode when you open the Appearance menu. Click on the option you want.

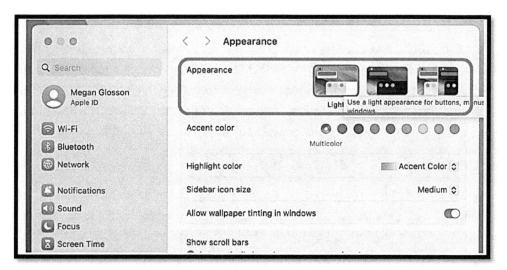

Change the Accent Color

You can select the accent color after you choose the mode. This will change the color that shows up when you select something or move through a menu. Select one of nine colors, then choose whether you want the highlight color to be the same as the accent color or different. Select the desired choices by clicking.

Change the Cursor Color

You can change the color of the cursor on your Mac desktop to make it look even better. Go to System Settings, then Accessibility, then Display. Choose colors for the Pointer Outline and Pointer Fill by scrolling down to Pointer. To fully change the color, click on the color swatch.

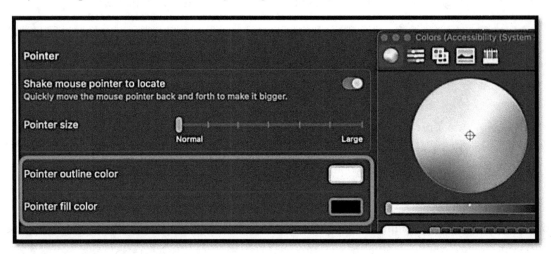

Replace Backgrounds in Finder

Replace the background that appears whenever you open a Finder window to further personalize macOS' look. Make sure Finder is set to Icon View first (from any folder, choose **View > As Icons**). After that, do these things: Open the folder you want to change in Finder, then go to the menu bar and choose **View > Show View Options**. Choose **Color or Picture** under the **Background** area. Selecting Color will launch the color picker while selecting Picture will launch a picture drop box.

Change the Start Page in Safari

Apple is finally letting users change the start page in Safari, after years of not letting them. You can change your background, Favorites, Siri Suggestions, Reading List, iCloud tabs, and your privacy report. Click on the Settings button in the bottom right corner of Safari to open a menu with many ways to change how the start page looks.

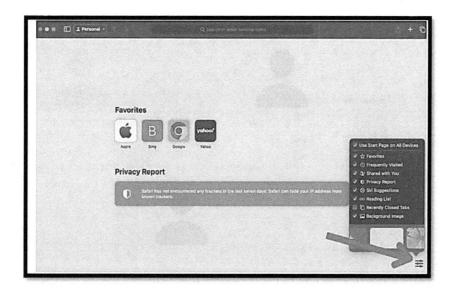

Most of the options, such as **Favorites** and **Recently Closed**, have a checkbox to click to add them to your start screen. To change the background picture, you can either pick one of the ones that are shown or press the plus sign (+) and select your image.

Personalize Individual Apps

With the most recent update to macOS, you can now customize more than just your desktop. You can also make some of the apps you use every day your own.

Some apps that you can customize are:

- To change your font and color settings in Apple Mail, navigate to Mail > Settings > Fonts & Colors.
- Terminal: To change the look, go to Settings > Profiles.
- TextEdit: To change how Dark Mode looks, go to View.
- Notes: To change Dark Mode, go to Notes > Settings.

How to change the brightness of your Mac

- The F1 and F2 keys can be used to change the screen's brightness.
- You can also go to the Apple menu, select System Settings, click Displays, and then click Display. To change how bright the screen is, slide the Brightness bar.
- For Intel MacBook Air models, press the F5 or F6 keys to change the color of the keyboard.
- Choose Control Center > Keyboard Brightness, then move the bar to the desired setting for Apple Silicon MacBook Air models.

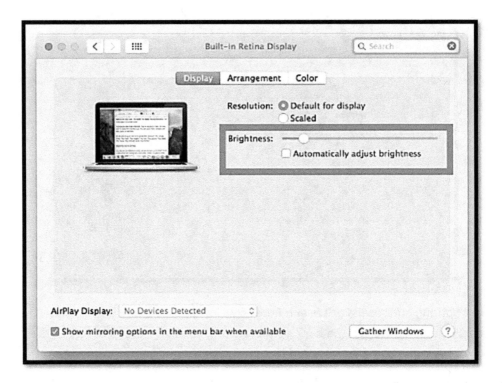

Changing the Volume of your Mac

- o   Click the Sound button in the menu bar or the Control Center.
- o   Slide the volume bar or use the Control Strip to change the amount.
- o   To get to the Sound control if it's not already there, go to the Apple menu and select System Settings. Then, click Control Center on the right.

Connect your Mac to WI-FI

1.   Click the Wi-Fi icon in the menu bar.
2.   Pick a network from the list of available networks.

3. Select Other Networks to see a list of nearby networks if the network you want to join isn't displayed.
4. If asked, enter the network password before clicking "Join."

Connect your Bluetooth device to your Mac

- The device's literature has more information on how to make sure it is on and can be found.
- In your Mac, go to the Apple menu and select System Settings. From the left, choose Bluetooth.
- Click Connect after moving the mouse over the device in the list.
- If asked, press Accept or type a string of numbers and press Enter.

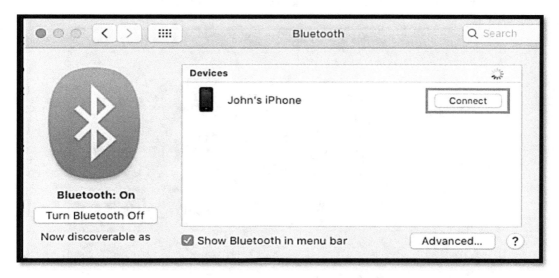

CHAPTER 3
MULTI-USER ENVIRONMENTS

In this chapter, we will look at how to create and manage user accounts, configure fast user switching, family sharing, setting up screentime, parental control, and how to manage apps.

Creating and Managing User Accounts

It can be hard to figure out how to use the user account system on a Mac, especially if you are new to macOS or are in charge of multiple users on the same device. It's important to know how to add, delete, and switch users when setting up a Mac for family use, a workstation in a business setting, or just to keep track of your personal and work-related tasks.

How to Add a User on Mac

The process of adding a new user to your Mac is easy and can come in very handy in many situations. macOS makes it easy and safe to set up an account for a family member, make a separate area for work, or just organize your digital life. After reading this article, you should be able to add a user to your Mac. This way, each user will have their own private and secure place on your device.

1. Open the System Settings app.
2. If you look to the left, scroll down and click on Users & Groups.
3. Click the "Add User" button on the right side of the box.

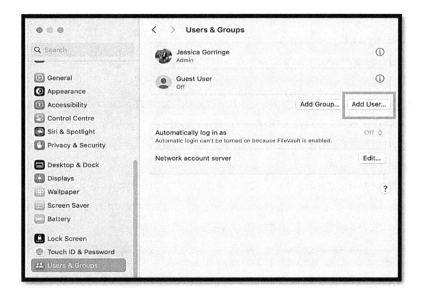

4. When asked, type in your Mac's Admin password.

5. To unlock, click the button.

6. Click the drop-down menu next to "New User" at the top of the new window.

7. Pick one of these options:

- **Administrator**: An administrator account can add or remove users, install or exit apps, change system settings, and more. You can make more than one administrator account on macOS. The Allow user to manage this computer setting can be used to turn a regular user into an admin user.

- **Standard** users can add or remove users and change their settings, but they can't install apps or change the settings of other users.
- **Sharing Only**: A user who is set to Sharing-only can only view your shared files from afar and doesn't need to log in to your Mac. In the Sharing options, you can change these settings in the File Sharing, Screen Sharing, or Remote Management panes.

8. Type in the user's full name.

9. The Account Name will be made immediately after the Full Name is entered. The Home Folder will still have the same name, but you can change it. To remind you, the Account Name can't be changed once the user is made if you don't change it.

10. Type in the new user's password. There must be at least four characters in your password, but you can leave the field blank if you don't want to use one.

11.Type in the same password again to make sure.

12. You can write a Password Hint if you think the new user might need it to help them remember their password.

13. To make a new user, go to the bottom right part of the window and click the Create User button. When you're done making the new user, you can change and enable a few more settings and options.

This is what you can do and how to do it:

- Open the System Settings app.
- If you look to the left, scroll down and click on Users & Groups.
- Next to the new user you just made, click the "Information" button.

- If you need to, click the switch next to **Allow this user to administer this computer** to "**On**."
- Press the **OK** button.
- Select the multi-select menu button next to **automatically log in as** at the bottom of the Users & Groups window.
- Select the account you want to sign in to automatically or select Off if you prefer to sign in by hand every time your Mac wakes up.

How to Add a Guest User on Mac

You can give friends, family, or coworker's brief access to your Mac by setting up a guest user account. This way, they won't be able to change your settings or data. When someone else needs to use your Mac, this function of macOS is very helpful for keeping your privacy and safety. Here are the easy steps you need to take to add a guest user to your Mac. This will protect your primary user's info and make it easy for other people to use your computer.

1. Open the System Settings app.
2. If you look to the left, scroll down and click on Users & Groups.
3. Just click on the "Info" button next to "Guest User."
4. Change the Username if you need to.
5. **You can turn on or off the following options:**
   - Allow guests to log in to this computer.
     - Enable the guest user so that friends can temporarily log in to your computer. Logging in to the guest account does not require a password. Users cannot log in to the guest account remotely. If FileVault is turned on, guest users can only access Safari.
   - Allow guest users to connect to share folders.
6. In the bottom right corner of the window, click the OK button.

How to Add a Group User Account on Mac

1. Open the System Settings app.
2. If you look to the left, scroll down and click on Users & Groups.
3. Click the "Add Group" button on the right side of the box.
4. Pick a name for the group in the window that pops up.
5. Press the "Create Group" button.
6. In the Groups area, next to the name of the group you just made, click the Information button.
7. Find the users you want to be a part of the group and click the toggles next to their names in the User Members area.
   - You can also change the group's name or get rid of it from this page.

8. Once you have chosen which accounts to add to the group, hit the **OK** button.

How to Switch Users on Mac

Enable Fast User Switching

It's helpful to have Fast User Switching turned on for your Mac because it lets you switch between user accounts quickly and easily without having to log out and back in. This is especially helpful if you share a computer or need to switch between different user profiles a lot for different tasks.

1. Do this on your Mac: Open the System Settings app.

2. Find Control Center in the list on the left side of the screen.

3. Scroll down to the bottom of the window on the right until you see Fast User Switching under "Other Modules."

4. To change this, click the drop-down choice next to Show in Option Bar.

5. **Pick one of these options:**
   - Don't Show
   - Full Name
   - Account Name
   - Icon

6. Turn on the Control Center by clicking the switch next to it.

Quickly Switch Between Users

- There is a Control Center button in the upper right part of the Menu Bar. Click it if you turn on Fast User Switching from there.
- Click the User button at the bottom of the Control Center
- Pick out the user you want to switch to from the window that comes up.
- If **Show in Menu Bar** was turned on, find the name or picture in the Menu Bar and click it.
- Pick out the user you want to switch to from the window that comes up.

How to Get Rid of a Mac User

1. Open the System Settings app.

2. If you look to the left, scroll down and click on Users & Groups.

3. Click on the user's name to the right of the "Information" button to delete them.

4. When the box comes up, click the Delete User... button.

5. Type in the admin password.

6. Click the Unlock button.

7. **Pick one of these options:**

        ○   Save the home folder in a disk image: The disk image is saved in the Deleted Users folder (in the Users folder).

             ○   Don't change the home folder: The home folder remains in the Users folder.

             ○   Delete the home folder.

8. Click the Delete User button when you're done making your choice.

9. Click the "Information" button to the right of the Guest User's name to "delete" them.

10. Click the toggle next to **Allow guests to log in to this computer** to the **Off** position.

11. In the bottom right corner of the window, click the OK button.

Setting Up Screen Time and Parental Controls

Activate Screen Time for Your Child

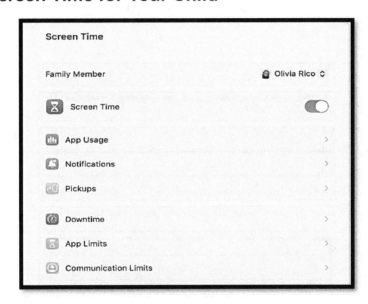

1. Select System Settings from the Apple menu.

2. Scroll down and click on Screen Time. Then, pick your child's name from the list on the right.

3. To add a child, click the button that appears on the right when you're using Family Sharing.

4. After you turn on Screen Time, do any of the following:

- **Include Website Data**: If you choose this choice, Screen Time reports will include information about the specific websites that were visited. Pages are only counted as Safari use if this option is not turned on.

- **Use Screen Time password**: If you choose this choice, you will need to enter a password to change Screen Time settings or make the time limits last longer.

Options for Screen Time on Mac

1. **App Limits**: You can control how much time you or your child spends on apps by setting time limits for certain apps or groups of apps. As soon as the limit is met, the app will not work again until the next day.

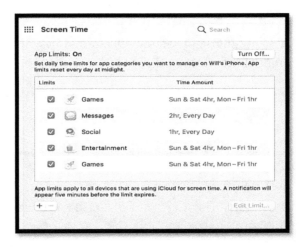

2. Through **Downtime**, you can set particular times when you won't be able to access certain apps or notifications. This can help you set tech-free zones or find a good balance between screen time and other activities.

3. **Communication Limits**: This tool lets you decide who your child can call, text, and FaceTime with. You can put limits on contacts or group chats to keep conversations safe and under control.

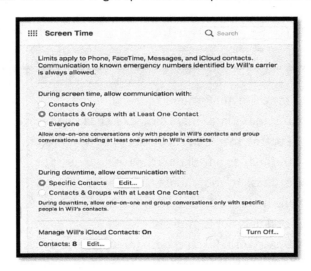

4. **Content and Privacy Restrictions**: You can block or limit access to adult content, certain websites, and other inappropriate things with Content and Privacy Restrictions. You can also control who can use the camera, microphone, or location services, among other things.

5. **Usage Summary**: Screen Time gives you a weekly summary of your usage habits, including how much time you spend on your phone, what apps you use, and how many notifications you get. This report gives you information about your online habits that lets you make smart choices.

6. **Notifications Management**: To cut down on interruptions and distractions, you can control and change the way alerts from different apps show up. Screen Time lets you pick which apps can send alerts and how they should act.

7. **Screen Time Passcode**: You can set a passcode for Screen Time to make sure that the settings can't be changed or rolled back quickly. This stops people who aren't supposed to be there from changing or accessing the Screen Time settings.

8. **App Usage Tracking**: Screen Time keeps track of how much time you spend on each app and gives you thorough reports. This app lets you see which apps you use most and how long you spend on each one.

9. **Always Allowed**: Let people use some apps even when the phone isn't working or when an app cap has been set for "All Apps & Categories." By default, Phone, Messages, FaceTime, and Maps are always allowed, but you can change that here.

CHAPTER 4

APPLICATION MANAGEMENT

In this chapter, we will walk you through app management. How to install and run apps, using split views, setting up dictation and Siri, and finally managing apps versions.

Installing and Running Apps

On your Mac, do any of the following:

- To open apps you got from the internet, go to the Downloads folder and double-click the disk image or package file that looks like an open box. If the installer doesn't open itself, you'll need to open it and then follow the on-screen directions.
- To use apps on a disc, put the disc into the optical drive on your Mac or a drive that is linked to your Mac.

Install apps on your Mac from the web

It takes a little more work to download an app from the web than from the App Store. You'll be able to use your new app right away if you follow these steps. If the file you downloaded ends in ".zip," you need to double-click it to open it. It will be possible to use the files.

The following steps must be taken if the file finishes in ".dmg":

- From the bottom left of your Mac's Dock, open Finder.
- From the window on the left, go to Downloads.
- Click the file twice to open it. Go to **System Settings** > Security & Privacy if you get an error message that says the program "can't be opened because it wasn't downloaded from the Mac App Store." To move forward with the installation, click the lock and press "Allow."
- As soon as you double-click the file, the app will be installed.
- If you use Finder, the app will show up in the Applications folder. You can remove the ".dmg" file from your computer by clicking the "eject" ⏏ button next to the app's name in Finder after installing it.
- You can add an app to the Dock by dragging its icon from the Finder's Applications area to the Dock.

Now your app should be all set to go.

Uninstall apps

You can get rid of apps that you installed or got from the web or a disc.

1. To get to Applications on your Mac, click the Finder button in the Dock and then click it.

2. **One of these things should you do:**
   - If the app is in a folder, open the folder and look for an Uninstaller. If you see Uninstall [App] or [App] Uninstaller, double-click it and then follow the on-screen directions.
   - Drag the app from the Applications folder to the Trash (at the end of the Dock) if the app isn't in a folder or doesn't have an Uninstaller.

The app will be gone from your Mac for good the next time you or the Finder empty the Trash. Some files that you made with the app might not be able to be opened again. Do not empty the Trash until you are sure you want to keep the app. Pick out the app in the Trash, then press File > Put Back.

Using Stage Manager

Stage Manager is a useful feature for switching between tasks that can be used on both Mac and iPad. As you work, it automatically arranges and groups open windows and programs, so you can focus on your tasks while still keeping an eye on everything. The way it does this is by showing images of your open windows on the sides of the screen and choosing one or more windows to take up the entire middle of the screen. This way, you can easily see if those screens have been updated or changed without having to open each one separately.

How to Turn Off and On-Stage Manager

There are two ways to turn on Stage Manager on your MacBook Air:

Option 1:
1. Pick up your MacBook Air and look for the Control Center button in the macOS menu bar.
2. Stage Manager can be accessed by clicking on the Control Center button.

3. There will be a window that pops up with a short description of the function and steps on how to use it.
4. To use the function, click the "Turn on Stage Manager" button.

Option 2:
- In the upper left part of your screen, click on the Apple menu.
- Choose "System Settings" from the list that comes up.
- To get to System Settings, open it and click on "Desktop & Dock."
- Get to the "Windows & Apps" tab in the Desktop & Dock settings.
- It should say "Turn Stage Manager on or Off."
- To use Stage Manager, flip the switch to the "on" position.

How to Use the Stage Manager

Do any of these things on your Mac:
- To **switch apps**, click on an app on the screen's left side.
- **Arrange windows**: Move, resize, and combine windows to make them work better for you.
- *Group apps:* Drag an app from the left side of the screen to the middle of the screen to add it to a **group of apps**.

- **Ungroup apps:** To take an app out of the group, drag it to the left side of the screen.

The list of apps on the left is not visible if "Recent applications" is turned off in Stage Manager settings. Just move the mouse to the left edge of the screen to see it.

Changing Stage Manager Settings on Your Mac

1. In the upper left part of your screen, click on the Apple menu.

2. Choose "System Settings" from the list that comes up.

3. In the window for System Settings, find "Desktop & Dock" 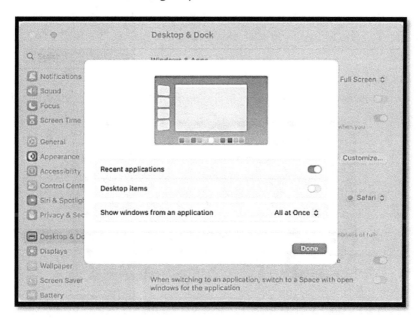 on the left side. You might have to scroll down to find it.

4. To change the Desktop & Dock settings, find "Windows & Apps" on the right side of the window and click on it.

5. Click the "Customize" button next to Stage Manager.

6. You can turn on or off the following settings in the personalization menu:

- **Recent applications**: If you turn this on, the most recently used apps will appear on the left side of your screen. If you move the pointer to the left edge of the screen, you can briefly see the recently used apps if this setting is off.

- **Desktop items**: If you check this box, things will appear on your desktop. The things on the screen will be hidden if this setting is off. When you need to get to something, you can click on the screen to bring it up.

7. The "Show windows from an application" menu will appear. From this list, pick one:

- **All at Once:** When you switch to this choice, all of an app's windows will be shown.
- **One at a Time**: This choice only shows the most recently used app window when you switch to it. This setting can be turned off, so you can click on the app on the left again to open the next window.

8. Once the settings are set up the way you want them, click "Done" to save your changes.

How to Use Split View

One useful feature of macOS that makes your life easy is Split View. You can see two windows at once on your Mac without them getting messed up or overlapping with other open windows. For Mac users who don't have an extra screen, Split View is a great way to use two apps at the same time. You can scroll through a document on one side of your Mac's screen while typing in Numbers on the other. This is called Split View. People who often do more than one thing at once on their computers will love this feature. There is one small problem, though: you can only use two apps at a time in Split View.

How to Split the Screen on a Mac

The Enter Full Screen button or Mission Control can be used on a Mac to split the screen. Both ways will be shown to you below.

Enter Split View on a Mac Using the Enter Full Screen Button

On macOS, most app windows have a "Enter Full Screen" button that lets you make them full-screen or tile them to the left or right half of the screen. This can be used to put an app in Split **View. Here's how:**

1. Start up the two apps you want to use together.

2. Move your mouse over the **green button** in the upper left area of the window for either app.

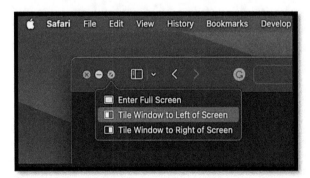

3. Choose the second or third choice from the context menu based on whether you want to snap to the **left or right**.

4. It's easy to tile the second app window, which shows up on the other half of the screen. Just click it.

Enter Split View on a Mac Using Mission Control

1. Start up the two apps you want to use at the same time.

2. **Bring up Mission Control:** The Mission Control (F3) key on your computer can be used to do this. You can also double tap the Magic Mouse with two fingers or swipe up with three fingers on your keyboard.

3. Place your mouse over an app window to the left or right of the blank space at the top of the screen and click on it. Drop the app window on top of the window with the plus sign (+).

4. Select the second app window and drag it to the empty spot. Then, drop it there to put it next to the first app in Split View.

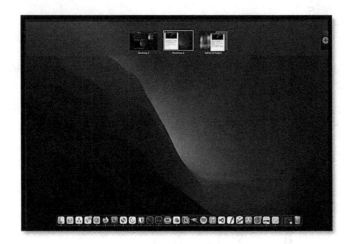

How to Adjust the Windows in Split View

After putting two apps on your Mac in Split View, here are some things you can do to make multitasking better.

Adjust the Split Screen Area

Simply click and drag the vertical line between the two windows to the left or right to make the window on either side of the screen bigger. In Split View, keep in mind that you can only change the sizes of the screens so much.

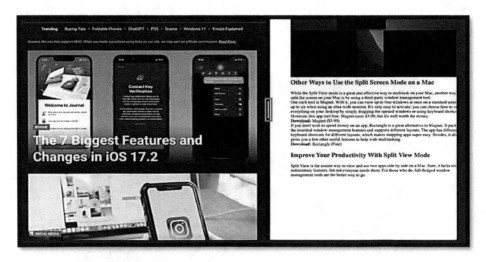

Switch Window Positions

You can easily move the window without leaving Split View if you think it would be easier to see one of the apps on the left side of the screen instead of the right (or the other way around). Press and hold the mouse button until it is at the top of the screen. In this case, the window's title bar will be shown. You can move an app to the other side of your Mac's screen by clicking and dragging its title bar.

Also, don't worry if you can't see the Dock on your Mac. When you're in Split View, it's secret. The Dock will appear when you move your mouse to the bottom of the screen.

Replace a Tiled Window in Split View

Now, if you want to use a different app than the two that are already open in Split View, you can switch out a tiled app window for a different one. To do this, go back to the desktop where the two apps are open next to each other. Select **Replace Tiled Window** by moving your mouse over the green button on the app window you want to change.

When macOS gives you a list of all the open apps on your desktop, click on the one you want to use. It will then appear next to the other app in split-screen mode.

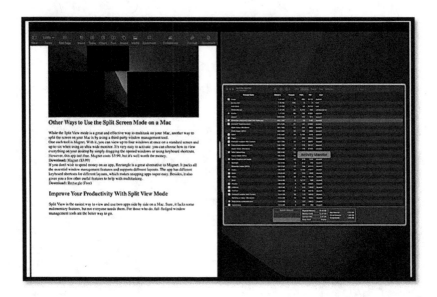

How to Exit Split View in macOS

On a Mac, you can get out of Split View mode in four different ways. Pressing the "esc" key is the best way to do it. The app you press the key on will leave Split View, and the other app will become full screen. But this way doesn't work for apps that do something else with the ESC key. You can also use the green button to leave Split View. You can choose what happens to the app windows when you leave Split View by moving your mouse over the green button and clicking on either **Move Window to Desktop** or **Make Window Full Screen**. It's possible that you can't see the **green button**. Press the top part of the screen.

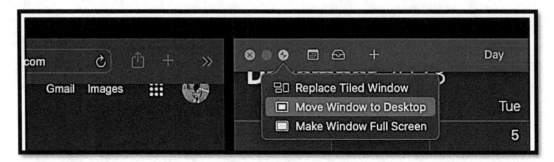

To close an app from the Split View screen, click **the** X button in the upper left part of its window. The other app will open in full-screen mode after you do this. Last but not least, you can also use **Mission Control** to leave Split View. Press the **Mission Control (F3) key** on your computer or use three fingers to swipe up on the trackpad to do this. Then, move the mouse over the space on the screen where the Split View windows are shown and click the arrows that point inward to separate them.

Setting Up Dictation and Siri

Use Siri on Your Mac

Follow these steps to make Siri work in macOS:

1. Start your Mac up and go to System Settings. From the menu on the left, choose Siri & Spotlight.

2. To use Siri, turn on "Ask Siri."

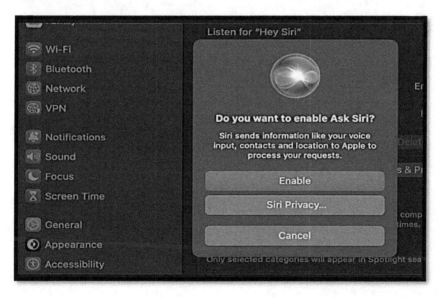

3. To use your words with Siri, you will need to turn on "Ask Siri." After you do this, Siri might ask you to say a few words so she can know your voice. That's it. You're now able to use Siri on your Mac. From the same page, you can also change your language and Siri's voice (accent).

How to Activate Siri on Your Mac

There are several ways to use Siri on your Mac after you have turned it on. You can use your voice to start Siri by saying "Hey Siri." You can also use the Siri button on your keyboard or in the menu bar of your Mac. You might be able to use the Siri button on the Touch Bar if you have a Mac with one. You can also use Type to Siri instead of saying out loud if you'd rather. We'll talk about these ways separately below:

1. Saying "Hey Siri"

The "Hey Siri" phrase is the most common way to get Siri to work. This needs to be turned on in System Settings under Siri & Spotlight. Turning on "Hey Siri," tells your Mac to listen for your voice and use Siri whenever you say the order. Siri will ask you to say a few words so that it can know your voice after you set this up. That's it! Now when you say, "Hey Siri," the Siri window will appear in the upper right corner, letting you use your helper.

2. From the menu bar

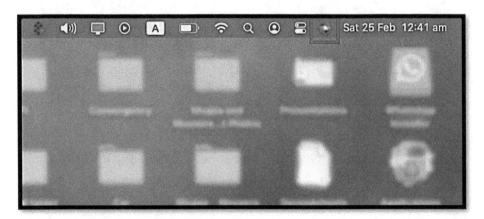

You can also turn on Siri by clicking the Siri button in the top-right area of the macOS menu bar. This way, your Mac will only listen for the "Hey Siri" phrase when you say it. If you're having trouble finding it, it's right next to the date. You can see Siri in the upper right area of your Mac. To use it, click the Siri button.

3. Using a Keyboard Shortcut

You can also use a keyboard shortcut to call up Siri, which you can set up in the Siri area of System Settings. You can choose one of the pre-set keyboard shortcuts or use the Keyboard Shortcut menu to make your own. This will let you tell Siri to start talking right from your Mac's keys.

4. Activate Siri with the Touch Bar

You might see the Siri button on the right side of the Touch Bar on a MacBook Pro. You can also use this instead of the Siri button in the menu bar to quickly call up Siri.

5. Type to Siri

By turning this on in the Accessibility section, you can "**Type to Siri**" instead of using your words to call Siri up through voice commands. Start by going to **System Settings > Accessibility**. Then, scroll down until you see Siri. If you turn on **Type to Siri**, you can type your Siri orders instead of saying them out loud. This is helpful when you're with other people and don't want to look awkward talking to Siri.

Use Dictation in macOS

I'm looking at how to use and set up Dictation for macOS. Some people may not know that Apple's macOS comes with voice recognition software that lets you dictate your voice straight into any text-based document. Dictation can be very helpful for people who would rather speak their thoughts than type them, in addition to being useful as accessibility feature. Not only does this keep you from having to buy dictation software from a third party, but Apple's version of dictation software also comes with some extra useful tools. Now that we have everything we need, I'll talk about how to use Apple Dictation with macOS and some of its benefits. This includes setting up the built-in speech software and using it the right way. I will also give you some dictation tips and talk about some other dictation choices. Because this can be very helpful for people who need disability features, I break down the steps so that everyone can understand what to do. I also talk about the most popular commands you can use with Dictation and some other commands as well.

What Is the Difference Between Voice Control and Keyboard Dictation?

People should know before they start that two different Accessibility features on macOS require you to talk to your computer. These two things are both very helpful, but they do different things. There are both words Control and macOS Dictation, which lets you turn your words into text. Voice run lets you turn your voice into text, and you can also use voice commands to run your Mac. The most important thing to know about Voice Control and Dictation is that Dictation will not work if Voice Control is turned on. You can use the menu bar to see if Voice Control is on by going to **Apple > System Settings > Accessibility > Voice Control** and making sure it is off.

How to Enable Dictation on macOS

If you want to know how to turn on Dictation on your Mac, just follow these steps. Keep in mind that if you have an Intel-based processor, you might need to be connected to the internet for the Dictation tool to work properly.

Follow these steps to make Dictation work on your Mac.

1. Get on your Mac and open the menu bar. Then, hit **Apple > System Settings**.

2. Scroll down to the bottom and select *Keyboard* from the sidebar.

3. Select **Dictation** on the right and make sure it is turned on. You might be asked if you want to share your voice records with Apple to make Dictation and Siri better. Choose what to do. In the next part, I explain what this means.

You are now ready to go! Dictation ought to be prepared. I will now show you how to use Dictation on macOS.

How to Use Dictation on macOS

You can start dictating text to your Mac now that Dictation is turned on. This is a great accessibility tool for people who need it.

To start a Dictation, just follow the steps below.

1. Select any Mac app and move the entry point to where you want to add text.
2. There are then three ways to start a Dictation:
   - Press and let go of the microphone button, which is in the row of feature keys and looks like a microphone.
   - You can also use the menu bar to go to **Edit > Start Dictation**.

   - Use a quick key combination. You can then use a special Dictation Key. In the menu bar, go to **Apple > System Settings** and then select **Keyboard** from the left. This will let you make a keyboard shortcut. After that, choose Dictation and click the menu icon next to the link. Then, from the drop-down list, you can pick one or make your Dictation shortcut.

3. An icon of a microphone will show up in the feedback window when your device is ready for Dictation. The microphone should move to show how loud something is. You might also hear a tone that lets you know your device is ready to allow you to dictate.

4. If you get either of these signs, you should start dictating. Keep in mind that this tool will add some punctuation marks, like commas, periods, and question marks, automatically. **Apple > System Settings > Keyboard > Dictation > Auto-punctuation** is where you can turn this off. People who use Apple hardware can add emojis by saying the emoji's name.

5. You can press the Return key to end your Dictation. You can also press a shortcut key or click "Done" in the feedback box. When your Mac doesn't pick up any words for 30 seconds, dictation also stops.

Dictation Privacy: What You Need to Know

People should know that if they turn on Dictation for the first time, their computer might ask them to share their voice recordings with Apple. If you agree, Apple will be able to save copies of what you type into Dictation. You can also use Siri instructions if you agree. If you agree, Apple can also listen to parts of your records. You can choose not to share this information. You can change this setting at any time by going to **Apple > System Settings > Privacy & Security > Analytics & Improvement > Improve Siri & Dictation.** This is true no matter what you choose when you first set up Dictation. This will stop Apple from keeping your Dictations and looking them over. If you use Dictation, on the other hand, Apple will listen to help them understand what you want. If you want to get rid of the records on your hard drive, all you have to do is go to **Apple > System Settings > Siri & Spotlight > Siri & Dictation History > Delete Siri & Dictation History.** Keep in mind that the Siri & Spotlight choice will only be called Siri on any OS before macOS Ventura. This can be a good way to get rid of your Dictation history and free up room on your hard drive.

Go Offline: Enhanced Dictation

It depends on the version of macOS you have that you may be able to use Enhanced Dictation. You'll know this is a choice on your Mac because there will be a box you need to check to make it work on the Dictation Settings page. Additionally, keep in mind that Dictation will not require an internet link if you are using a Mac with Apple hardware. This can be very helpful for people who do a lot of work offline. By going to **Apple > About This Mac,** you can always find out whether your chip is Apple or Intel. You have an Intel-based Mac if you see the word "Intel" anywhere in the Processor area.

Tips for Effective Dictation on macOS

If you are using Dictation on a Mac, you might want to learn more about the speech recognition software tool before using it all the way. This app can help if you use it for a long time because it helps your Mac understand your voice better. The more you use the tool, the more accurate it will become. When using Dictation, you should also think about your voice and the speech that works with it. If you speak clearly and at a steady pace, your accuracy rates will keep going up. Don't forget to follow the rules for spacing as well. You might need to use the Dictation feature a few times before it works perfectly, but taking the time to get better at it will only make things easier. If you find that you have used Dictation for a long time or are unhappy with the results, you might want to look into getting a more advanced microphone. You might also want to get rid of any sounds or distractions in the background.

Utilize Dictation in Various Languages

One good thing about Apple Dictation is that it comes in a lot of languages, though the exact list will change from Mac to Mac. For instance, a Mac with Apple chips is likely to have more language choices than a Mac with Intel chips. You can change the language of Dictation by going to **Apple > System Settings > Keyboard > Dictation** and choosing a language from the Language drop-down menu. You can pick a language from the list or click **Customize** or **Add Language** to add more. Most likely, English will be the usual choice. The usual setting may also depend on the language you picked when you set up your Mac in the first place.

You can get rid of languages too. Just open the Language pop-up menu, choose Customize, and uncheck any languages you don't want to use. It's also important to know that you can dictate in more than one language. As long as the function is set up to work with more than one language, you can choose the language you want to use from the feedback window.

Dictation and App Compatibility

Any Apple app that is built for macOS will work with Apple Dictation without any problems. This might not be the case for third-party apps, though. There are probably a lot of apps that will work, but some might not. These could be popular apps. If you find that Dictation doesn't work with a different app, keep in mind that the program might not support this option. To see if an app has any information about this function, you can also look at the App Store page for that app. You might want to use your favorite app in a certain setting, but keep in mind that macOS apps may work better with the feature than third-party apps.

Dictation in Siri

Apple's voice recognition software is built into Dictation, but don't forget that Siri can also be your helpful virtual helper. iOS 7's virtual helper, Siri, has been around since October 2011 and can be very useful on its own. You can think of Siri as a good mix of Voice Control and Dictation. Siri can't do everything that these features can do, but it can do much of what they can do well. You can use Siri to send texts by saying, **"Hey Siri, send a message to."** It can also help you remember things and do other things.

Differences in Enabling Dictation on Different macOS Versions

The steps for turning on Dictation may be written differently in different versions of macOS, but they should be mostly the same. To get to the Keyboard, just use the menu bar to go to **Apple > System Settings**. Find Dictation and make sure it's turned on. You might get different prompts in different versions of macOS, but the steps are always the same. Just remember where the Dictation setting is and make sure it is turned on, whether you are using macOS High Sierra or Sonoma. Keep in mind that System Settings may be called System Preferences in older versions of macOS. Pay attention to the words.

How to Fix Dictation Issues: Issues and Fixes

Voice Control and Dictation will not work simultaneously, which is something the user must keep in mind. You can have one or the other. Make sure that Voice Control is turned off by going to **Apple > System Settings > Accessibility > Voice Control** and making sure that it is turned off. If that doesn't help, try turning on Dictation again. Pay attention to your settings for accessibility. You may also have trouble with your computer picking up your voice. Even though I talked about this earlier, I think it's important to stress again that you might need to spend some time with Dictation to get it just right. It might need some practice before it's perfect. Additionally, keep in mind that Dictation will add a blue line to text that isn't clear. If the program thinks a sentence isn't clear, you can click on the blue-highlighted text and make the changes that the Dictation suggests. You can also speak or type your changes. One thing you might want to think about is getting a new microphone if Dictation has been making mistakes for a while now. Also, keep in mind that while you are using Dictation, you might not be able to hear sounds from other apps. But this one is simple to fix. If you don't hear any sound from any of your apps, you can either press the Return key or wait 30 seconds without speaking to have Dictation close on its own.

CHAPTER 5
FILE AND FOLDER MANAGEMENT

Keeping your files and folder is important to help you navigate through any files when needed. In this chapter, we will walk you through file and folder management. We will look at how to navigate the file system, using the finder tabs, stacksm tabs, and managing files.

Navigating the File System and Finder

What is Finder on Mac?

Finder is a built-in app in macOS that lets you work with your Mac's file system. It's the same thing as Windows' File Explorer. You can move files, folders, and other things in Finder. You can also copy and delete them. With Finder, you can also run programs and connect to resources on the network. The Finder icon looks like a blue happy face. In the Dock, you can always find it.

You can't get rid of Finder even though it's an app. On a Mac, SIP protects it, and it has more rights than any other Apple default app in macOS. When you're in the Dock, you can't hide or move Finder around.

How to open Finder on Mac?

Click the **Finder** icon in the Dock to open the Finder window. There will be a window where you can look through your files and groups. If you press **Cmd+N**, you can also open Finder. But click on any space on your screen before you press these keys. This link opens the desktop app that is currently running in a new window.

How to open two Finder windows on Mac?

If you want, you can put as many Finder apps on your desktop as you want. There are several ways to do this:

Way 1

In the Dock, right-click on the Finder icon and choose "New Finder Window."

Way 2

Choose File > New Finder Window from the menu bar is another way to open more than one Finder window.

Way 3

The macOS has quick tools for the things you do most often. The shortcut below can be used to start a new Finder window:

Press Cmd+N

New Smart Folder may be shown in both the context menu and the drop-down menu. This brings up a more detailed Finder search window where you can narrow down the results to only the kinds of things you want to see.

How to open a new tab in Finder on Mac

It's easier to work with tabs than to start a lot of Finder windows. Right-click on a folder and choose "**Open in New Tab**" from the menu that comes up. This will open the folder in a new tab. You can do this with folders in the window and files on the left side of Finder.

How to explore files on Mac?

Mac provides two options to find something in your system:

- Spotlight search
- Finder search

The search tools Spotlight and Finder are not the same. Spotlight lets you search for a word in contacts, dictionaries, mail, messages, the Internet, and other places. The Finder search, on the other hand, only works for files and folders. Spotlight can't find things that are hidden. You can look through even secret files and folders in Finder.

The Finder app on your Mac lets you look through files and groups. Finder is a lot more than just a window with folders and files in it. It's everything on your computer.

Finder search

In Finder, the search box is in the upper right corner. Press Enter after typing the name of the file or folder you want to find.

Finder searches the whole Mac by default, but you can change the settings to change how it searches. How to do it:

1. Open Finder.
2. In the menu bar, click Finder and select Preferences.
3. Switch to the Advanced tab.
4. **Select one of the following options for search performance:**
   - Search this Mac
   - Search the current folder
   - Use the previous search scope

New Smart Folder

You can look through files in Finder not only by their names but also by other criteria. With the New Smart Folder in Finder, you can do this. Just right-click on the Finder icon in the Dock and choose "New Smart Folder" to open it. You can also use the Finder menu to open a New Smart Folder.

To find files on a Mac, use Smart Folder in this way:

- Open a new smart folder.
- Press the plus sign (+).
- Pick out the type of file you want to see.
- Set up other options, such as the size, name, extension, and so on.
- Press "Enter" or "Return."

Note: Finder doesn't show the Mac path for files by default. Sometimes, it can be hard to figure out where a file is stored and how to get to a certain area. To always see the whole path, navigate to the **Finder** menu, click **View**, and then choose **Show Path Bar**. Then, you can quickly get to one of the folders in the path by double-clicking on it.

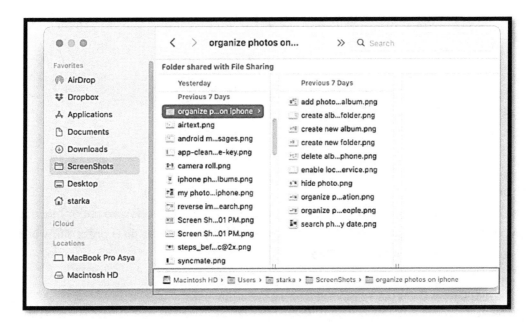

You can also right-click on a file and choose "**Get Info**" to get its address. You can see where the file is saved in the Info panel.

Managing Files or Folders in Finder

1. Create a New Folder with Selected Files

Maybe you have a bunch of pictures or papers that need their box. The easy way or the better way is how you can do this.

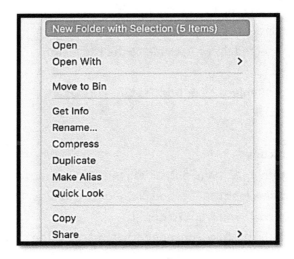

In the old days, you would make a new folder and then drag and drop the files inside it. The way this is done is pretty easy, but it could be easier.

Instead, you can follow these steps to pick out all the important files and have them make their new folder:

- Pick out each important file.
- Go to the File menu or Control-click any file you've chosen.
- Choose **New Folder with Selection**.
- Type in the name of the new folder.
- Type "Enter."

Now your things will go to the new folder that you made.

2. Cut or Move Files in Finder

Making copies and pasting is pretty simple in Finder, but it's not clear how to cut or move things. Luckily, this function is easy to use once you know how. **All you have to do is press a few buttons. Here's how to cut or move things in Finder:**

- Pick out the file you wish to move.
- Press **Cmd + C** or **Edit > Copy** "File name" to copy.
- Find your way to the desired location.
- You can use **Cmd + Option + V** to move the file, or you can hold down the Option key and click the Edit menu, then choose Move Items Here.

You can see that Finder doesn't have a cut choice. However, moving does the same thing.

3. Rename Several Files

You might need to change the names of more than one file at the same time sometimes. Most of the time, you would handle each file one at a time, but sometimes batch renaming is more efficient. You can change the text, add text, or choose your style.

Here's what you need to do to rename several files in Finder:

1. Pick the relevant files.
2. Control-click any selected file or navigate to the **File** menu.
3. Pick **Rename**.
4. Pick a rename type: **Replace Text**, **Add Text**, or **Format**.
5. Complete all fields.
6. Click **Rename**.

4. Change File and Folder Icons

Sometimes you want something to stand out, or you might be a chaos agent who wants to throw someone off by making folders look like files and files look like folders. **This is how you can change icons in Finder, no matter what you want to do:**

1. **Copy** an item with the desired icon, or another image, to the clipboard.
2. Pick the file or folder you want to change.
3. Control-click the item or navigate to the **File** menu.
4. Pick **Get Info**.

5. Tap the icon in the **Get Info** window.

6. Paste with **Cmd + V** or **Edit > Paste**.

The picture you pasted should now show up where the icon used to be. To use a picture, you'll need to open the file and copy the picture. That's what will show up when you paste if you only copy the picture.

5. Use Tags to Color Code

Using tags is a great way to keep track of things. First, color-tagged things are easy to find in long lists. Second, the search function in Finder lets you find files that have the same tags. To tag something, do these things:

1. Select the relevant item.

2. Click the **Edit Tags** icon in the Finder's control bar, Control-click the pick, or go to File.

3. Pick out the tags you want.

To find files that have been tagged, type the name of the tag (red, blue, important, etc.) and then click on the option that shows up below the search box.

6. Make Smart Folders.

Smart folders are a good way to keep track of things automatically. Say, you could set settings that say all PNG files with "screenshot" in the name should go to a certain folder. When you add more things to your Mac that have the same variables, macOS will add them instantly to the other files. **To make a smart folder, do these things:**

1. Navigate to Finder's **File** menu.

2. Tap **New Smart Folder**.

3. Type the desired parameters into the **Search** box.

4. Pick the desired variables.

5. Tap **Save**.

6. Enter a folder name and location.

7. Click **Save**.

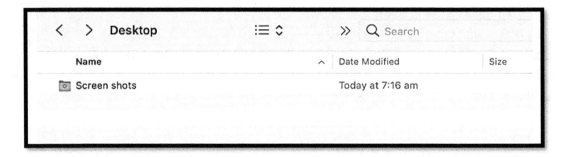

The main feature here is automation, and you can set multiple conditions and make smart files that are pretty complicated when you need to.

7. Lock Folders

When more than one person uses the same login, or when you often delete files by mistake, locking folders can be helpful. If you try to remove something from a locked folder, you will be asked for the admin password. Until the folder is unlocked, you will not be able to add anything new. **This is what you need to do to lock a folder:**

1. Pick the relevant folder.
2. Control-click or navigate to the **File** menu.
3. Choose **Get Info**.
4. Tick the **Locked** box in the info window.

When you need to, you can uncheck the box to unlock the folder.

8. Compress Files

macOS has a compression tool that can be used for more than one thing. To begin, as the name suggests, this function shrinks files by putting them into a ZIP archive. Second, the tool lets you quickly join several things, which come in handy when you need to send a lot of attachments.

Follow these steps to compress your files:

1. Pick all relevant files.
2. Control-click or navigate to **File**.
3. Tap **Compress**.

The zipped files will show up as Archive.zip, but you can change the name if you need to.

9. Check and Access the Folder Structure

It might seem like an easy tip to be able to go to other places within the current folder structure, but it's not clear how to do this. **In macOS, take these steps to see and get to the folder structure:**

1. In the Finder's control bar, Control-click on the name of the present folder.

2. Pick out the folder that you want to see in the layout.

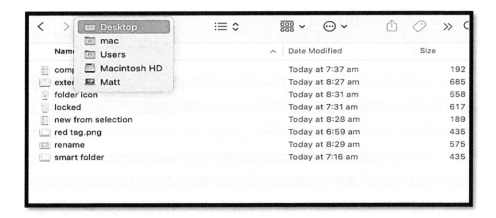

That's it. Simple but useful, this tip can save you a lot of time if you have to go from one place to another a lot.

10. Show or Hide Filename Extensions

It can help to be able to see the title of a file if you need to change its name. The extension can get in the way sometimes, though, and make changing things a pain. You can change how Finder shows file names, which is good in macOS. To change the settings for all files, follow these steps:

1. Finder > Preferences > Advanced is where you need to go.

2. You can choose to show or hide all file extension options.

Here's how to change the settings for just one file:

1. Select the appropriate file by using Control-click.

2. Use the Control-click or File menu to get to the Get Info page.

3. Mark or clear the "Hide extension" box.

You could always find out more.

Even though Finder is easy to use, not all of its useful features are clear at first glance. Putting things you've chosen into new groups makes filing easy, and knowing how to cut or move files can save you time and work. macOS also has a tool called "batch rename" that helps you name larger groups of files, and smart folders and tags make it easy to find things. One more useful feature is the ability to lock files and change icons for good or bad reasons. Also, the macOS compression tool makes files smaller and easier to send to other people. One more useful feature is the choice of whether to show or hide file names. Lastly, a great way to save time is to Control-click on the name of the present location to see the folder structure.

Use Finder Tabs

Through Finder's Tabs, you can keep several folder windows open at once without making your screen too crowded. You can even switch files between tabs, which make it easy to find things quickly.

How to Use Tabs in macOS Finder

Open the Finder app by hitting its icon in the dock. Then, to use tabs, press the tab key. You might not be able to see your tab bar in the first Finder window that comes up. Click "**View**" at the top of the screen and choose "**Show Tab Bar**." You can also press **Shift+Command+T** on your computer to show the tab bar. You can skip this step if you see "**Hide Tab Bar**" in the "**View**" menu instead. This means that the tab bar is already shown.

It is near the top of the Finder window, just below the toolbar, when the tab bar is shown.

The plus ("+") button can be used at any time to add a new Finder tab. You can also use the keyboard to press Command+T. Click on the tab you want to see in the tab bar to switch between them. To close a tab, all you have to do is click the "X" button that shows up in the tab when you move your mouse over it. You can also use the keyboard to press Command+W.

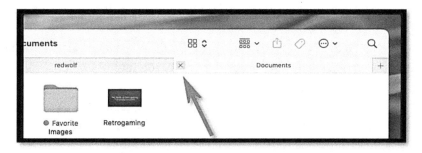

To move a file or folder to a different tab, just drag and drop it there. Each tab in this case works a lot like a shortcut to the place it points to. You can also open as many tabs as you want in Finder. In an open window, if there are more open tabs than the width of the tab bar, the tab titles will scroll to the side. If you click on the far left or right ends of the tab bar, you can move between them. Have fun finding!

Use Stacks to Keep Your Desktop and Dock Organized

It can be very difficult and time-consuming to find a single file on a Mac desktop that is overflowing with documents, folders, images, PDFs, and other files. Stacks, on the other hand, let you quickly arrange your files with just a few clicks. On a Mac, you can use Stacks in two places: on your screen and in the Dock. Both will clear up your workspace and make your papers easier to find and organize.

How to Use Stacks on Your Desktop

You can use Stacks on your Mac to order the files on your desktop by putting them into groups based on what they have in common. You can, for example, choose to stack your desktop files by type. This will put all of your photos, PDFs, spreadsheets, and other types of files together.

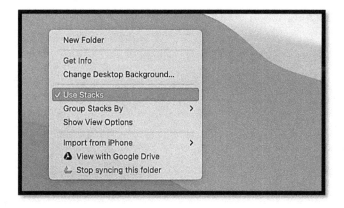

It's very easy to use Stacks on your PC. Press and hold the Control key on any spot on your desktop, then choose "**Use Stacks**" from the choice that comes up. Immediately, this will arrange your files on the right side of your screen in groups based on their type. The same thing can be done by hitting **Control + Cmd + O** on the keyboard if you'd rather. You can change how the stacks are grouped by holding down the Control key and moving your mouse over **Group Stacks By**. This will show you different sorting choices, such as by date or by the tags on the documents. Single-click on the stack icon to open it up and see what's inside. You can also open a file by double-clicking on it in the stack. Keep your mouse over the stack sign and swipe left or right with two fingers on a trackpad or one finger on a Magic Mouse to see what's inside without opening the stack.

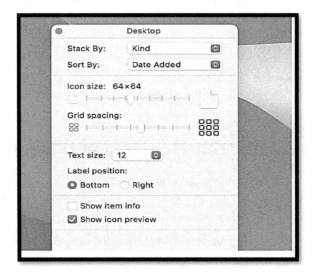

You can also change how the stacks on your screen look. In the menu bar at the top of your screen, find **View** and click on **Show View Options**. The size of the icons and the distance between stacks are two settings that you can modify in the pop-up menu.

How to Use Stacks in Your Dock

You can also use Stacks with files in the Dock of your Mac. A popular way to use this feature is to add the Downloads folder to the Dock so that you can quickly get to files you've recently downloaded.

To do this, open Finder and look for Downloads. Then, drag and drop the whole folder to the right of the line that separates them into the Dock. If you **Control-click** on the Downloads folder in the Dock and choose **Display as > Folder**, you can change the icon to the original folder. By default, the icon will look like a stack of papers. Now, to change how the folder's contents are shown when you click on it, Control-click on it in the Dock, and under "**View content as**," choose a style like "**Grid" or "Fan**." When you open a file, the Grid view lets you see more of them. The Fan view is mostly used for stacks in the Dock. Of course, the Downloads folder is just one popular way that the Stacks feature in your Mac's Dock is used. You can, of course, add any other folders to your Dock in the same way to make it easy to get to the files they hold.

Organization with Stacks Is Quick and Convenient

One very useful thing about your Mac is the Stacks function. It not only clears up your desk, but it also sorts your papers into useful groups so you can find them quickly when you need to. Plus, with just two clicks of your mouse or trackpad, your computer's files are nicely organized and easy to find. That's one of the easiest ways to keep your digital life in order. Additionally, while Stacks is a quick and easy way to organize your computer's files, there are many other techniques and methods you might want to use to keep your files organized and simple to find.

CHAPTER 6
WEB AND EMAIL

The built-in Safari web browser on the MacBook Air M4 is a crucial component of the macOS power brought right to your fingers. Web browsing and email handling can be much improved by learning the ins and outs of Safari, regardless of experience level with Macs. The MacBook Air M4's Safari is vital for personal and business use because it is built for speed, efficiency, and privacy. Safari has a plethora of capabilities to delve into, ranging from organizing your bookmarks to proficiently handling tab groups, and from personalizing your browsing with extensions to safeguarding your online privacy. Additionally, Safari's easy integration with your email accounts simplifies the process of managing your digital communications. You can easily manage your inbox by organizing, filtering, and searching through emails, and it comes with built-in support for the most popular email providers.

This chapter walks you through every aspect of utilizing Safari on the MacBook Air M4, including important subjects like:

- **Web Navigation with Safari**: here you will learn the fundamentals of web browsing, such as how to manage your history, open, close, and arrange tabs, as well as how to make use of Safari's intelligent search capabilities.
- **Customizing Safari:** you will get the latest information on how to manage your extensions, change security and privacy settings, and use the Reader mode to read without interruptions to make your Safari experience more unique.
- **Using Safari with Email**: You will gain more insights on how to use the built-in capabilities in Safari for effective email handling, as well as how to manage your inbox and integrate your email accounts with the browser.

This chapter will help you get the most out of Safari on your MacBook Air M4, making it your go-to tool for everything email and web-related. It includes straightforward instructions and helpful advice.

Using Safari: Customizing and Navigating

On macOS, Safari is the default web browser. You can greatly improve your surfing experience by getting to know its features. Regardless of your level of experience with Macs, knowing how to successfully modify and use Safari can help you get the most out of it.

Change your homepage

Any webpage can be set as your homepage, appearing whenever a new tab or window is opened.

- Select **Safari**

Preferences

From within the Safari software on your Mac, then select **General.**

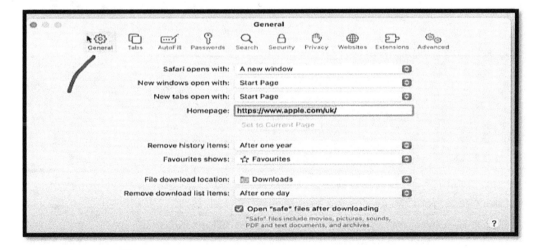

- Enter the address of a webpage in the Homepage area. Click **Set to Current Page to use the webpage you are currently reading.**
- Select the time when your homepage appears.

Select **History > Home** in Safari to open your homepage quickly.

Customize a start page

The start page is a handy location to gather all the information you value most from the internet.

- Select **Bookmarks**

> Show Start Page from the Mac Safari program.

- In the window's lower-right corner, select the **Options button.**
- Choose the **start page options.**

85

- Open the Start Page on Every Device: If you choose this, your iPhone, iPad, iPod touch and other Mac computers will all utilize the same start page settings. You need to have iCloud configured for Safari and be logged in to all of your other Apple devices using the same Apple ID as on your Mac. Additionally, all of your Apple devices need to have two-factor authentication enabled. Refer to the Apple ID two-factor authentication article in Apple Support.
- Tab Group Favorites: Display the URLs you've added to the chosen Tab Group as favorites.
- Recently Closed Tabs: Display URLs from recently closed tabs within the designated Tab Group.
- Favorites: Display web pages from the bookmarks folder you selected under General.
- Frequently Visited: List the websites you have recently or frequently visited.
- Shared with You: Using the Messages app, view links, videos, and other content that friends have shared with you. Make sure Safari is chosen in the Messages settings' Shared with You tab to view items in Shared with You. In the Contacts app, you can only see content shared with you by others who are in your contacts.
- Siri Recommendations: Provide recommended websites from Mail, Messages, and other apps. You can activate Siri Suggestions if it's not listed.
- Reading List: List the websites you have chosen to read at a later time.
- Privacy Report: Display a summary of your privacy, on which you can click to learn more about who was unable to follow you.
- iCloud Tabs: Display open websites on other Apple devices. To access Safari on your other Apple devices, you need to have iCloud set up and be logged in with the same Apple ID as on your Mac.

- Drag the start page options into the desired order of appearance.
- In the Safari window, click.

The start page can show up each time a new window or tab is opened. Refer to Modify General Preferences. By clicking in the **Smart Search area, you can also view the start page.**

Create a profile

By making a profile for each aspect of your life, you can keep your browsing distinct from your browsing for work, education, and other purposes.

- Click **Create Profiles** after selecting **Safari > Settings in the Mac Safari program.**

Click New Profiles if this is your first profile.

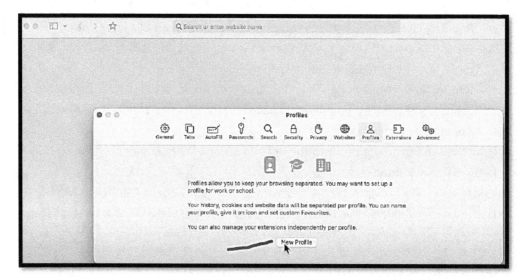

- Under the list of profiles, select the **Add button.** This is the last step you need to do if this is your first profile.
- Give this profile a name, and then **select a color and icon.**
- In this profile, select **a favorites folder containing your preferred websites.**
- To create a profile, click **Create.**

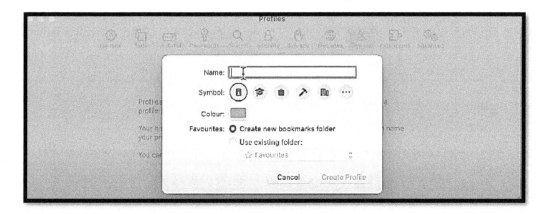

- To choose which extensions to use with this profile, click **Extensions.**

Note however that passwords stored in iCloud Keychain can be accessed from any profile you create. You always have a Personal (Default) profile in addition to any profiles you establish. Your personal profile's name, icon, and color can all be altered.

Change profile settings in Safari on Mac

You can create and configure browsing profiles in the Safari program on your Mac by going to the Profiles settings and selecting what opens in a new window or tab when you open a profile. Select **Safari > Settings, then click Profiles to modify these options.**

Option	Description
Profiles list	a list containing the default profile together with the profiles you've made. To create a profile, select the Add button beneath the list. To delete a profile, select the Delete button located beneath the list.
Name	Insert a preferred name for the profile
Symbol	Choose an icon for the profile
Color	Select a color of your choice for the profile
Favorites	To save your preferred websites in your profile, select the bookmarks folder.

New windows open with	Select the content that opens in new windows while you use this profile.
New tabs open with	Select the tabs that open when you use this profile.
Extensions	Choose the extensions you would like to make use of with the profile

Block pop-ups

Pop-up windows may be annoying or useful. On certain websites, you must permit pop-ups. Your monthly statements, for instance, can appear as pop-up windows on a bank website. Pop-up advertisements from other websites could cover your screen. Pop-ups can be disabled or allowed on certain websites, or all websites. If you're not sure if you want to block pop-ups on websites, you have the option to block them, get warned when the website tries to show one, and then select whether or not to show it.

Allow or block pop-ups on one website

- Open the website in your Mac's Safari program.
- Select **Websites after selecting Safari > Settings.**
- On the left, click **Pop-up Windows.** Make careful to scroll to the bottom of the list if Pop-up Windows isn't visible.
- **Select any of the following from the website's pop-up menu:**
  - **Give permission:** The website's pop-ups open.
  - **Block and Notify**: When you access a website with prohibited pop-ups, you may choose to view them by selecting the Show button located in the Smart Search field. Otherwise, pop-ups for the website do not appear.
  - **Block:** The website's pop-ups are not visible.

Allow or block pop-ups on every website

- Click Websites after selecting **Safari > Settings in the Mac Safari program.**
- On the left, click **Pop-up Windows. Make careful to scroll to the bottom of the list if Pop-up Windows isn't visible.**
- Choose **each website**, then click **Remove** if there are any listed below-Configured Websites that you would like to change their settings (for instance, they are set to Allow, but you would like to change them to Block). If you don't see Configured Websites, you've

either cleared the list of websites to block pop-ups or you haven't set up pop-up blocking for any yet.

- **Select one of the following options when the "When visiting other websites" pop-up menu appears:**
  - **Permit:** The websites' pop-ups show.
  - **Block and Notify**: When you access a website with prohibited pop-ups, you may choose to view them by selecting the Show button located in the Smart Search field. Otherwise, pop-ups for the website do not appear.
  - **Block**: The websites' pop-ups are not visible.

If a website's pop-ups are blocked but they still appear, your Mac may be running undesired software. Note: You might not be able to view some information if you ban pop-ups.

Make Safari your default web browser

The default browser on your Mac initially comes with Safari installed. You may quickly reset your default browser to Safari in case you unintentionally changed it or simply want to go back to it.

- Select **System Preferences from the Apple menu on your Mac, then click Desktop & Dock from the sidebar. (You might have to scroll below.)**
- Select **Safari** from the pop-up option that appears next to "Default web browser" on the right.

Certain applications launch websites in a browser apart from your preferred one.

Browse the Web

The MacBook Air M4 comes pre-installed with Safari, which offers a seamless and user-friendly browsing experience. It combines cutting-edge features like configurable start pages, sophisticated tracking prevention, and seamless connection with other Apple services with speed. Safari's user-friendly interface makes it easier for all users, novice or expert, to browse and manage their favorite websites.

Go to a website

You can easily visit the websites you wish to visit with Safari.

- Enter **the name or URL** of the website in the Smart Search area of the Safari software on your Mac. Safari Suggestions display as you write.
- Select **one of the suggested addresses or hit Return to go straight to the address you typed.**

Bookmark web pages to revisit

A bookmark is an online link that you store for easy access at a later time.

Add a bookmark

- Navigate **to the website you wish to bookmark using the Mac's Safari application.**
- Select **Add Bookmark** after clicking **the Share icon in the toolbar.**

- **Select the bookmark's location and, if desired, give it a new name.**
  - ○ Include this page to select a folder by clicking the option that appears. Favorites are the default.
  - ○ Change the bookmark's name: To make the website easier to find, enter a short name.
  - ○ Include a description: As an optional reminder about the webpage, add further information.
- Select **Add.** Additionally, a bookmark can be added in the Smart Search field: Point the cursor over the Smart Search box, then select a bookmarks folder from the list by clicking and holding the One-Step Add button that shows up at the left end of the field. You can locate the bookmark in the sidebar after adding it.

Locate a bookmark

- Select the **Sidebar button** in the toolbar of the Safari application on your Mac, then select **Bookmarks.**
- In the search bar at the top of the sidebar, **type the name of the bookmark.** It might require scrolling to make the search field visible.

Use a bookmark

- Select **the Sidebar button** in the toolbar of the Safari software on your Mac, then select **Bookmarks.**

Alternatively, pick **Bookmarks > Show Bookmarks.**

- In the sidebar, click **the bookmark.** It is also available through the Bookmarks menu.

Manage bookmarks

- Choose **the Sidebar button in the toolbar of the Safari software on your Mac, then select Bookmarks.**
- You can control-click a folder or bookmark.
- Select **one of the following actions from the shortcut menu:**
  - Edit or rename a folder or bookmark. In addition, you can click the name with force or click and hold it until it highlights before typing a new one.
  - Modify the URL (website address) of a bookmark.
  - Delete or copy a folder or bookmark.
  - Make a folder for bookmarks.
  - View the contents of the folder in detail.

Double-clicking a folder in the sidebar, followed by a control-click on the item, will allow you to alter the bookmark's description. The option **Bookmarks > Edit Bookmarks** allows you to manage bookmarks as well.

Note: If you have iCloud set up for Safari on your Mac computer, iPhone, iPad, or iPod touch, Safari will use iCloud to maintain your bookmarks across devices. Your reading list and bookmarks are automatically saved by iCloud, and you can always restore them from a previous version.

Delete a bookmark in Safari on Macbook Air M4

When a bookmark is no longer needed, it can be deleted.

- In the Mac Safari application, select **Bookmarks from the toolbar by clicking the Sidebar button.**
- Select **Delete after doing a control click on the bookmark.**

See your favorite websites

By adding websites to your Favorites, you can easily view the ones you visit often and access them with a single click.

- Point the cursor over the Smart Search area in the Safari software on your Mac.
- Select **Favorites after clicking and holding the One-Step Add button that shows up at the left end of the field**. Alternatively, you can **click in the Smart Search field and drag**

the website's URL to the Favorites area on the start page, the Favorites folder in the sidebar, or the Favorites bar at the top of the window.

Note: If you sign in with the same Apple ID on all of your Apple devices, you can maintain your favorite websites. Make sure Safari is turned 'ON' on your iPhone, iPad, or iPod touch by going to **Settings > [your name] > iCloud**. Make sure Safari is turned 'ON' on your Mac by selecting **Apple menu > System Settings, clicking [your name] at the top of the sidebar, clicking iCloud on the right, and then clicking [your name].** To enter or create an Apple ID if you don't see your name, click Sign in with your Apple ID. You may have removed the bookmark for a preferred website from one device if it is absent from another.

Use tabs for web pages

Do not overload your desktop with Windows when you are conducting research or browsing the web. Tabs allow you to see many web pages in a single Safari window instead.

Preview a tab

Point **the cursor over a tab in the Safari application on your Mac.**

Open a new tab

- Choose the **New Tab button located in the toolbar of the Safari software on your Mac, or utilize the Touch Bar.**
- Select **Safari > Settings, click General,** click the **"New tabs open with" pop-up menu, and then select an alternative website to open in new tabs.**

Open a webpage or PDF in a new tab

Using the Mac's Safari program, choose one of the following actions:
- Command-click **an icon in your Favorites or a link on a webpage.**
- Using the Back or Forward buttons on the command line, navigate to the previous or next webpage in a new tab.
- Enter text into the Smart Search area, and then use **Command-click to select an item from the list of suggested searches, or Command-Return.**

Select **Safari > Settings, click Tabs, then uncheck the box next to "⌘-** and it will click open a link in a new tab" if you want to use these command-key shortcuts for opening web pages in new windows rather than tabs.

Open a webpage in a new tab from the bookmarks sidebar

Using the Mac's Safari program, choose one of the following actions:
- Control-click **a bookmark** to bring up the shortcut menu, then select **Open in New Tab.**

- To open a bookmarks folder in new tabs **control-click on it.** In the folder, every bookmark opens in its tab.

Click the **Sidebar button in the toolbar, and then select Bookmarks to open the bookmarks sidebar.**

Open a tab in another window

- You can either select **Window > Move Tab to New Window** or drag t**he tab across the desktop in the Mac version of the Safari software.** Additionally, you can drag a tab from one Safari window to another's tab bar.

You can only move tabs within private windows to other private windows. Only to other non-private windows may tabs in non-private windows be moved.

Automatically open web pages in tabs

- Select **Safari > Settings from within the Safari software on your Mac, and then select Tabs.**
- Select **an option after clicking the "Open pages in tabs instead of windows" pop-up menu:**
  - **Never**: Hyperlinks that open in a new window open in fresh windows.
  - **Automatically**: Links that are meant to open in new windows automatically open in new tabs.
  - **Always**: Links that are meant to open in separate windows with specific formatting always open in new tabs. This also applies to links that are meant to open in new windows.

Reopen a recently closed tab

- Select **the webpage** you wish to revisit by selecting **History > Recently Closed** in the Safari program on your Mac. Reopening a closed tab or window is another option.

Import bookmarks, history, and passwords

You can import your bookmarks, history, and passwords automatically when you first start using Safari, or you may import them manually at a later time if Google Chrome or Mozilla Firefox is your regular browser. Additionally, bookmarks exported from Mozilla Firefox, Microsoft Edge, Google Chrome, and a few other web browsers can be imported. Moreover, you can import credentials that were exported from a password app or another browser into a CSV file.

- Your current bookmarks are displayed before imported bookmarks.
- Your current history is displayed alongside your imported history.

- Your iCloud Keychain stores imported passwords, allowing you to automatically fill in login credentials on websites.

Instantly import from Chrome or Firefox

- On your Mac, open the **Safari application.** You'll get a notification at the bottom of the start page asking you if you wish to keep imported items if this is your first time using Safari after using Google Chrome or Mozilla Firefox.
- Choose a choice:
    - **Save your imported items:** Safari preserves the passwords, history, and bookmarks you import from Chrome and Firefox.
    - **Delete the objects you imported**: Safari deletes the items you imported.
    - **Make a decision later:** Go back to the home screen and import the things later. Select **Bookmarks > Show Start Page to view the start page.**

Manually import items from Chrome or Firefox

- Select **File > Import From > Firefox or File > Import From > Google Chrome** in the Mac Safari app. Even if you have previously imported things, you can still do this at any point once you launch Safari. To import, you need to have Firefox or Chrome installed on your Mac.
- Choose **the objects that you wish to import.**
- Select **Import.**

Import a bookmark file

- Select **File > Import From > Bookmarks HTML File** in the Mac Safari program.
- To import, select **the HTML file.**
- Select **Import.**

Once you import bookmarks, they show up in a new folder called "Imported" and conclude with the date in the sidebar beneath Bookmarks.

Import a password file

- Select **File > Import From > Passwords CSV File** in the Mac Safari application.
- To import, select the **CSV file.**
- Select **Import.**
- Enter your Mac's login password here. If the password you're importing doesn't match the one you've saved to your Mac, you can select which of the relevant accounts, user names, and passwords to maintain by seeing them all.
- Choose **Delete "filename.csv"** for the protection of the security of your accounts.

WARNING: Your passwords are visible to anyone viewing the CSV file since it is not encrypted.

Export a bookmark file

- On your Mac, select **File > Export > Bookmarks from the Safari software**.

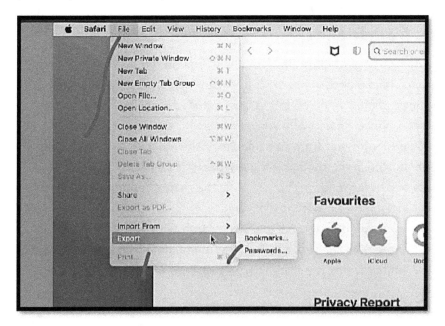

The file that was exported is named "Safari Bookmarks.html."

- Import the "Safari Bookmarks.html" file to utilize the exported bookmarks in a different browser.

Export a password file

- On your Mac, select **File > Export > Passwords from the Safari software.**
- Select **"Export Passwords."** Please note that: A CSV file containing your passwords is exported. Your credentials are visible to anybody who opens the CSV file because it is not encrypted.
- After g**iving the CSV file a name and location,** click **Save.**
- Enter your Mac's login password here.
- Import the CSV file you made to utilize the exported passwords in a different browser.

Read articles

You may use several extensions and built-in features in Safari to improve your reading experience and productivity. In this section, you will learn more about the number of things you can do when reading articles with the use of your safari application.

View links from friends

You may see what friends send you in Shared with you on the Safari sidebar when they use the Messages app to share videos, news articles, or other links. (Ensure that Safari is chosen in the Messages settings' Shared with You tab to view items in Shared with you). In the Contacts app, you can only see anything shared with you by those who are in your contacts.)

- Click **Shared with you from the sidebar of the Safari software on your Mac (click the Sidebar button in the toolbar if the sidebar isn't visible).**
- Choose one of the following actions from the shared content list:
  - In Safari, click **content to view it.**
  - To respond to the person who shared with you through Messages, click their name. Click t**he name displayed immediately below the toolbar to respond while reading the story.**

Keep a Reading List

Add webpages to your Reading List to conveniently bookmark them for later reading. You can save webpages from your Reading List to read them offline—that is, without an internet connection.

Manage your reading list

Using the Mac's Safari program, choose one of the following actions:

- Place **your cursor** over the **Smart Search box and click the One-Step Add button** that shows up at the left end of the field to add a webpage to your reading list. To add a web page quickly, you can **also Shift-click a link on another webpage.**
- To display or conceal your reading list, select **Reading List from the toolbar after selecting the Sidebar button.** Click the **Sidebar button once again to conceal the list.**
- Put a webpage in your Reading List to be read from an internet connection: Select **Save Offline by controlling-clicking the webpage summary in the sidebar.** Alternatively, you can click **Save Offline** after swiping leftover the webpage summary. Go to **Safari > Settings, click Advanced, then enable "Save articles for offline reading automatically" to have all webpages in your reading list automatically saved.**
- Delete a page from your list of books: Select **Remove Item by controlling-clicking the webpage summary in the sidebar.** Alternatively, you can click Remove after swiping left

over the webpage summary. Alternatively, swipe left until the webpage summary vanishes.

Read from your Reading List

Using the Mac's Safari program, choose one of the following actions:
- **Look through your reading list:** Type text into the search bar located above the summary of web pages. It might require scrolling to view the search field.
- **Examine the following page in your list**: When you get to the conclusion of a Reading List webpage, keep scrolling instead of clicking the sidebar's next webpage summary.
- **Hide the pages you have visited:** Above the list of summaries of web pages, select Unread. To view the web pages you've read in your list, click **the All button**. To see the buttons, you might need to scroll.
- **Check if a web page has been read or not**: The webpage summary in the sidebar can be control-clicked to select Mark as Read or Mark as Unread.

Keep in mind that Safari leverages iCloud to maintain the consistency of your Reading List across Mac computers, iPhones, iPads, and iPod touches that have iCloud configured for Safari.

Hide ads when reading

With Safari Reader, you can read an article on a webpage all on one page that is easy to read and free of distracting elements like adverts and navigation. For Reader, you can change the font, font size, and background color.

View an article using Reader

- Choose the **Reader button in the Smart Search area** of the Safari software on your Mac. The button appears only if there is a post on the webpage that the Reader can display.
- Press **Esc or click the Reader icon once again to exit Reader.**

Change how your web pages look in Reader

- Click the **letter button that shows up at the right end of the Smart Search field** in the Safari software on your Mac when you are viewing an item in the Reader view.
- **To change the settings, do any of the following:**
    - Select **the font size.**
    - Select **a background that is white, gray, sepia, or black.**
    - Select **a typeface.**

The font, size, and background you last selected are always displayed to you by Reader.

Take notes

When using Safari to read a webpage, you can take notes, copy content from the webpage, and paste the webpage link into a Quick Note without ever leaving the browser.

Jot down ideas about a webpage in a note

- Navigate **to a webpage using your Mac's Safari software.**
- Hit the **keys Fn and Q.**
- Type **text** in the appearing Quick Note.

Copy text from a webpage to a note

- Open **the webpage in your Mac's Safari application.**
- Choose **a text.**
- Press and hold the text, then select **Add to Quick Note**. Safari highlights the content and a link to the URL displayed in the Quick Note. Your highlight remains visible when you return to the website, and a thumbnail of the Quick Note shows in the bottom-right corner of the screen.

Paste a web page address in a note

- Open **the webpage in your Mac's Safari application.**
- Click Share, then select **Quick Note > Add to Quick Note.**

Like regular notes, Quick Notes can be edited. Move the pointer to the Quick Note hot area, which is usually the lower-right corner of the screen, and then click **the note that appears to reopen the note.** To ensure that a new Quick Note is always started instead of being added to, open the Notes program on your Mac, select **Notes > Settings, and then uncheck the box next to "Always resume to last Quick Note."** Your Quick Notes are located in the Notes app's Quick Notes folder.

Translate a webpage

You can ask Safari to translate a webpage if it can be found in one of your favorite languages.

Translate a webpage

- Navigate to the webpage you wish to translate using your Mac's Safari program. The Translate button appears in the Smart Search area if the webpage is translatable.
- Select **a language by clicking the Translate button**. Click the **Translate button and select Report Translation Issue if you believe the translation may use some work. Apple receives the translation for evaluation.**

If a language is not available

By adding the languages in the Language & Region settings, you might be able to expand the number of languages available in the Translate menu. If a language has a translation after you add it to your list of preferred languages, it shows up in Safari's Translate menu. Note: Depending on the nation or location, translations may not be available in all languages or all languages.

Download and Save Content

With the use of the safari program, you can download and also save content you like from various web pages you visit. In this section, you will learn how to download content from the web and also design a PDF of web pages from any website you visit.

Downloads items from the web

You can download files from webpages, such as software, audio, and PDFs, by simply **clicking links.**

Important: When you open an item that you downloaded, you will see a notice if it contains software. If it's not from a reputable source or you weren't expecting software, it's best to avoid opening it.

Download an item

- Click **any link that appears to be a download in the Safari software on your Mac, or Control-click an image or other element on the page.**
- Select "**Download Linked File.**" (Some items on the webpage cannot be downloaded.) After downloading files, like.zip files, Safari decompresses them.

Note: To save space on your Mac, Safari eliminates older duplicates when you download an item that you have already downloaded.

Try any of these suggestions if you're having problems downloading:

- Wait for Safari to finish downloading the item if it is still in progress. An item cannot be opened while it is downloading.
- Resume the download if it has been paused. Click the Show Downloads button to display the list of downloaded files, and then choose the Paused download and click Resume.
- There are situations when a download fails because the file is corrupted. Try downloading it once more.
- Verify that you have the application required to open the file. If so, there's a chance the file was damaged during download. After deleting it, try downloading it once more.

See items you have downloaded

- On your Mac, open the Safari software and select the Show Downloads option located in the upper-right corner of the Safari window. If the download list is empty, the button is hidden.
- **Take one of the following actions:**
  - To stop a download, click **the Stop button in the downloads list, which is located to the right of the filename. Click the Resume button to start over.**
  - On your Mac, locate a downloaded item: In the downloads list, click **the magnifying glass icon next to the filename**. After a file has been downloaded, moving it or changing its download location will prevent Safari from finding it.

Advice: Select **Safari > Settings**, click **General, then click the "File download location" pop-up menu and select a place to modify where downloaded files are saved on your Mac.**

  - **Remove items from the downloads list**. Select **Remove from List after Control-clicking the item to remove it**. By default, after a day, Safari deletes an item automatically. Select **Safari > Settings**, open **General,** then click the **"Remove download list items"** pop-up menu and select an option to modify the time at which objects are automatically deleted.

The file you downloaded can be a disk image or a compressed archive with the desired file in it. Double-clicking the file will cause it to decompress if it is from a reliable source. You can open an app by bypassing security settings if you download it and receive a notification stating that it cannot be opened because it was not obtained from the Mac App Store or is from an unrecognized developer.

Add passes to Wallet

To add passes, like movie tickets or boarding cards, to Wallet (also known as Passbook) on your iPhone, iPod touch, or Mac, use Safari. Safari on your iPhone, iPod touch (iOS 6 or later), or Mac, needs to be configured with iCloud.

Add a pass to the Wallet

- On your Mac, open the **Safari software and select Add to Wallet in the pass**. Click **Update** if the pass has previously been added but its contents have changed.

View a pass

- Click the **webpage link for the pass in the Safari software on your Mac.** The pass has been used or is expired if the barcode is muted. Click **the Info icon** in the pass to view details.

Share a pass

- Choose the **Share button** in the pass within the Safari software on your Mac.
- Decide how the pass will be shared. Select **Apple menu > System Settings, click Privacy & Security in the sidebar, then click Extensions on the right to select which items show up in the Share menu. (You might have to scroll below.)**

If Mirror iPhone is enabled in the Apple Watch app, adding a pass to your iPhone also adds it to your Apple Watch's Wallet. To enable Mirror my iPhone, open the Apple Watch app, select My Watch, then select **Notifications > Wallet & Apple Pay.**

Save part or all of a webpage

A webpage can be saved in its entirety, complete with all of its links and images, or just sections of it.

Save text from a webpage

Drag the text you've selected in the Safari app to the desktop or another document on your Mac.

Save an image from a webpage

- On your Mac, Control-click **the image in the Safari program.**
- Select "**Save Image to "Downloads**." Choose to **Add Image to Photos or Save Image As.**

Certain photos cannot be preserved, such as background images. Certain photos allow you to drag them straight to your desktop or a document.

Save a link from a webpage

You can **drag a link from the Safari program on your Mac to a document on the desktop**, or you can **control-click the link and select Add Link to Reading List or Add Link to Bookmarks.**

Save a whole webpage

- Select **File > Save As from within the Safari application on your Mac.**
- Select **Format > Page Source or Format > Web Archive.**
    - Web archive: Maintains all visuals, and links function as long as the webpages they lead to are accessible. For transient pages, like receipts, web archives are helpful.
    - Saves only the HTML source code for this page. If you wish to utilize the HTML source for your webpage, this is helpful.

Print or create a PDF of the webpage

You can display the site address and date in headers and footers, as well as the webpage's background image and color when printing or printing a PDF of the webpage.

- Select **File > Print from within your Mac's Safari application.**
- Select **Safari from the options pop-up menu (seen in the divider bar), then adjust the webpage printing settings.**

Select **Show Details at the bottom of the Print dialog box if you are unable to see the options pop-up menu in a divider bar to the right of the page preview.**

Choose **PDF at the bottom of the dialog box to make a PDF of the webpage, then select the desired action for the PDF.**

Save a document as a PDF on a Mac

A document that has been saved in Portable Document Format (PDF) can be shared with others. If someone has a PDF viewer, like Preview or Adobe Acrobat, they can read the document even if they don't have the tool you used to produce it.

- Open the document you wish to save as a PDF on your Mac.
- Select **File > Print.**
- To access the PDF pop-up menu, click the **PDF button or the down arrow, then select Save as PDF.**
- Give the PDF file a name and location. Fill in the Title, Author, Subject, and Keywords fields with the desired information. Spotlight can be used to do a later search based on the data entered into those fields.
- Click **Security Options to set a password to safeguard your document.** Passwords may be necessary to access the document, copy content from it, and print it.

You can save your receipt as a PDF instead of printing it if you made an online purchase and the webpage is displaying it as proof of purchase. Select **Save to Web Receipts from the PDF pop-up menu after clicking it. The PDF file is now located in your Documents folder's Web Receipts folder.**

Interact with text in a picture

You can use Live Text to deal with words and numbers by selecting the text in an image or photo. You can send an email to an address or receive a map of an address, for example.

- Navigate to a picture or image that displays text in the Mac's Safari software. The text may consist of words, a physical address, a website address, a phone number, or an email address.
- Select the text by dragging the pointer over it.

- To pick a text, control-click on it.
- **Choose from the following options:**
  - **Copy:** Select the Copy option. The text can then be pasted into another document or application.
  - **Get a definition**; Select Look Up to get a definition.
  - **Translate**: To translate, select Translate [text] and then a language.
  - **Note**: Not all languages have translation available and not all nations or areas may have it.
  - **Do an online search**: Select Use [web search engine] to search.
  - **Give to others**: Select Sharing, and then select the text's sharing method.
  - **Call or send a message**: You have the option to give the number a call, begin a FaceTime audio or video chat, or send a message. Moreover, you have the option to click the down arrow that shows up when the pointer passes over the phone number.
  - **Send an email.** Select whether to initiate a FaceTime audio or video call, compose an email, or add the email address to Contacts. When the pointer passes over the email address, another option is to click the down arrow that displays.
  - **Visit the following website:** To access the information on the website, click the link or utilize Quick Look in your browser. When the pointer lingers over the website address, you have the option to click the down arrow that displays.
  - **View the map**: Show the street address when you launch the Maps app. If you drag the pointer above the street address, you have the option to tap the down arrow that appears.

Setting Up and Managing Email Accounts

You can send, receive, and handle emails from all of your Mac accounts in one place by using the Mail program. All you have to do is connect your current accounts to Mail, including iCloud, Exchange, Google, school, work, and others.

Add your first email account to Mail

When you launch Mail for the first time, you might be prompted to add an account. Email account domains are shown in the dialog.

- Choose Another Mail Account or another account type. Note: Choose iCloud if you wish to add your @iCloud, @me, or @mac address.
- Enter the details for your account.

You can utilize an account you currently have on your Mac for other programs, like Messages or Contacts, with Mail. To access the Internet Accounts settings in Mail, select **Mail > Accounts, and then click the Add Account button on the right.**

Add more email accounts to Mail

You can add extra email accounts even if you've already added some.

- Select **Mail > Add Account from Mail.**
- Choose **a kind of account.**
- Enter **the details for your account.**

Hide your email address

By subscribing to iCloud+, you can register for services and complete forms online without disclosing your actual email address.

- Choose the email address field in the Safari software on your Mac when a website requests it.
- Select "**Hide My Email**." It is advised to use a distinct, random email address. Your actual email address receives emails sent to the address.
- **Take one of the following actions:**
  - Obtain a new email address: Press the Refresh icon.
  - Click Use to use the recommended email address.

Manage cookies

All of the websites that have saved cookies and website data on your Mac are visible to you, and you have the option to delete part or all of it.

- Select **Privacy from the Safari app's Settings menu on your Mac.**
- To manage website data, click **Manage.**
- Choose **Remove or Remove All after selecting one or more websites.** Eliminating the data might lessen tracking, but it might also cause websites to log you out or behave differently.

Note: Clearing cookies and website data in Safari may cause other apps to modify or delete them as well.

Clear your browsing history

You can erase all traces that Safari retains of the websites you've visited over a specified duration. Your browsing history gets erased from all of your Apple devices—including your Mac—if you have iCloud set up for Safari on them. Any surfing histories maintained separately by the websites you visited are not cleared when you delete your browsing history in Safari.

- Select **History > Clear History from the Safari app on your Mac**

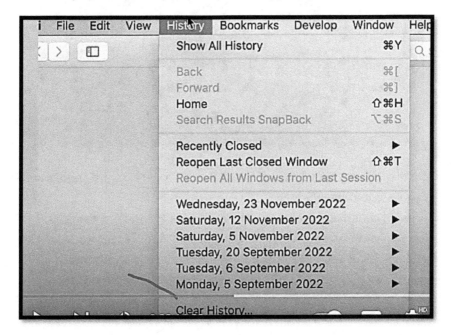

And then choose the pop-up menu.
- Select the extent to which you wish to delete your browsing history.

Safari deletes information it saves from your browsing when you clear your history, including:
- History of web pages you visited
- The back and forward list for open web pages
- Frequently visited site list
- Recent searches
- Icons for web pages
- Snapshots saved for open webpages
- List of items you downloaded (downloaded files aren't removed)
- Websites added for Quick Website Search
- Websites that asked to use your location

- Websites that asked to send you notifications

Browse Privately

When you browse in private, neither the websites you neither view nor the data of your browsing activity are shared with your other Apple devices.

- Select **File > New Private Window from the Safari software on your Mac**

 Or open an existing private browsing window. There's a dark Smart Search area with white lettering in a private browsing window.

- **Proceed with your usual browsing. While utilizing Private Browsing:**
  - Websites you visit are unable to trace your surfing across several sessions since browsing started in one tab is segregated from browsing started in another tab.
  - You do not save your AutoFill information or the web pages you visit.
  - You cannot see your open webpages while viewing all of your open tabs from other Apple devices since they are not saved in iCloud.
  - Whenever you use the Smart Search field, the results list does not contain the searches you have recently performed.
  - The downloads list does not contain the items you download. (The contents are still there on your PC.)
  - Private browsing windows are not sent to your iPhone, iPad, iPod touch, or other Mac computers if you utilize Handoff.
  - You cannot store changes to your cookies or website data.

Given that websites are unable to alter data saved on your Mac, services that are typically offered at these websites can function differently unless you utilize a non-private window.

Note: If you have any open non-private Safari windows, none of the following applies.

Stop browsing privately

- You can open a non-private window in the Safari software on your Mac by choosing **File > New Window, exiting the private window, or switching to a non-private window.**
- Take any of the following actions to improve privacy even more:
  - Anything you downloaded using private windows should be deleted.
  - If you have any other private windows open, close them so that nobody else may view the web pages you visited in those windows by using the Back or Forward buttons.

"Use advanced tracking and fingerprinting protection" is activated by default when you use Private Browsing. This setting removes known tracking parameters from all URLs and prevents connections to data collection organizations that employ sophisticated fingerprinting techniques (a method of identifying your device based on data obtained while you browse). Activating sophisticated tracking and fingerprinting protection may have an impact on certain website functions. Select **View > Reload Reducing Privacy Protections if the website you are reading is impacted.** In addition to using private windows, you may control cookies and data that are saved on all websites, stop cross-site monitoring, and more. You can delete your surfing history if you neglect to utilize a private window.

Prevent cross-site tracking

Certain websites make use of outside content suppliers. You can block third-party content providers from following you around websites to promote goods and services.

- Select **Privacy from the Safari app's Settings menu on your Mac.**
- Choose **"Don't allow cross-site tracking."** Their website data and cookies are removed unless you visit and engage with the third-party content provider as though it were a first-party website.

Share, like, and Comment buttons are frequently added by social networking platforms to other websites. Even if you don't utilize these buttons, they can still be used to monitor your online activity. Safari prevents such tracking. You will be prompted to grant the website access to view your actions on other websites if you choose to continue using the buttons.

Note: whenever you access a website, it collects information about your device, including system setup, and utilizes that information to display content that is optimized for your device. This information is used by certain businesses to attempt "fingerprinting," or uniquely identify your device. To avoid this, Safari shows a condensed version of your system settings each time you visit a page. Because your Mac looks more like everyone else's, trackers have a far harder time identifying your laptop.

See who tried to track you

Whenever you visit a website, you can see who has been barred from tracking you.

- Enter the name or URL of the website in the Smart Search area of the Safari software on your Mac.
- From the toolbar, select the **Privacy Report button.**

Select **Safari > Privacy Report to view** a list of known trackers that have been prohibited from tracking you.

Change settings in Safari on Mac

To customize your internet browsing experience, use the Safari settings. Select Safari > Settings from the Safari app on your Mac, then click one of the options panes:

- **General:** Modify your homepage, select which bookmarks to display in the Favorites view, decide where to save downloads and for how long, and decide what to see whenever you open a window or tab.
- **Tabs**: Select whether to use keyboard shortcuts, place tabs onto the toolbar, and decide when you want to display web pages in tabs.
- **AutoFill:** Choose to have previously saved credit card information automatically entered on webpages, usernames, and passwords entered when returning to websites, and contact information automatically filled out on forms.
- **Passwords**: You may view, add, modify, delete, and share the passwords and usernames you've saved for websites.
- **Search**: In Safari, choose which search engine to use and whether to use the Smart Search area to assist with searches.
- **Security**: Accept websites' usage of JavaScript and receive a warning if you visit a website that looks to be phishing.
- **Privacy**: Avoid being tracked by third-party content providers on other websites by deleting any or all of the cookies that are saved on your Mac.
- **Profiles**: Make your browsing profiles and select what opens in a new window or tab within a profile.
- **Extensions**: Installing Safari extensions from the Mac App Store allows you to alter the appearance of site content, add custom controls, and much more.
- **Advanced:** In the Smart Search field, display complete website addresses; configure advanced privacy settings; and display functionality for web developers.

CHAPTER 7
COMMUNICATION TOOLS

A variety of communication features are included with the MacBook Air M4 to enable smooth communication, whether you're interacting with friends, family, or coworkers. The MacBook Air is a flexible and dependable tool for all your communication needs, whether for personal usage, business endeavors, or educational purposes, thanks to these features and the potent capabilities of the M4 chip. This chapter will teach you how to use these resources to your fullest potential so that you stay in touch with the people you care about.

Configuring and Using Messages

Send an infinite number of messages to anyone logged into iMessage on an Apple device with an Apple ID by using iMessage, a secure messaging service. IMessage-sent messages show up as blue text bubbles. You can use your Mac to send SMS messages to any mobile phone, provided that your iPhone is running iOS 8.1 or later. SMS messages show up as green text bubbles.

Get messages on your Mac with the use of iMessage

- Insert **your Apple ID and password in the Messages program** on your Mac, and then select **Sign In.**

- Ensure that you log in to all of your devices using the same Apple ID.
- Visit the Apple ID account website if you need to create an Apple ID or if you've forgotten your password.
- Select **Messages > Settings, choose iMessage, pick Settings, and then choose any of the options below**;
  - To store your messages in iCloud, turn on the **"Enable Messages in iCloud" option.** Note: The iCloud settings allow you to enable or disable Messages in iCloud.
  - **Messages can be directed to you at**: Decide which phone numbers or email addresses you want people to use to contact you.
  - **Send read receipts**: Tick this box to let others who send you messages know when you've responded. Additionally, read receipts for a particular chat can be sent.
  - **Launch new discussions from** Select the phone number or email address you wish to use to initiate new discussions. You can only use this option if you have multiple phone numbers or email addresses listed beneath the "You can be reached for messages at" line. Note: whenever you send a message, people see this information. When you have your phone number chosen, for instance, it appears in interactions with other people.

Send a message on Mac

Once you've configured Messages on your Mac, you may send messages with text, images, animation effects, and more to an individual, a group of individuals, or an organization.

One can express themselves in a variety of ways:

- **Tapbacks**: See Use Tapbacks.
- **Photos and videos:** See Send photos and videos.
- **Stickers and images:** See Send stickers, Use #images, and Create your Memoji.
- **Audio messages**: See Send an audio message.
- **Message effects:** See Use message effects.
- To begin a new message in the Messages program on your Mac, tap the **Compose button (or utilize the Touch Bar).**
- In the designated To field, provide the recipient's name, email address, or phone number. Messages propose addresses as you type, either from contacts in your Contacts app or from people you've messaged before. In addition, you have the option to click **the Add button to the right of the To area.**

After selecting a contact from the list, click the phone number or email address. Notice: An hourglass icon will show up next to the names of the persons you are unable to message if you are only able to send and receive messages with specific individuals.

- In the space provided at the window's bottom, type your message. If accessible, you can use the typing suggestions.
- On your keyboard, press **Return to send the message.**

To respond inline and maintain a more structured discourse, go to send an inline reply to a message. See Send a message or attachment to forward a message. See Unsend or amend a message if you discover that you made a mistake in your message. By using your Game Center account to send a message, you can extend an invitation to new players for multiplayer games. Because your communications are end-to-end encrypted, not even Apple can read them—only you and the recipient can do so. Use Contact Key Verification to confirm that you are communicating with the individuals you intend to communicate with.

Send a message to a group

- To begin a new message in the Messages program on your Mac, hit **the Compose button (or utilize the Touch Bar).**
- For each recipient you wish to send a message to, enter their name, email address, or phone number in the To field. Messages propose addresses as you type, either from contacts in your Contacts app or from people you've messaged before. In addition, you have the option to click **the Add button to the right of the To area**. After selecting a contact from the list, click **the phone number or email address.**
- **In the space provided at the window's bottom, type your message. If accessible, you can use the typing suggestions.**
- On your keyboard, press **Return to send the message.**

Send a message to a business with Business Chat

You can send messages to specific businesses if you're running macOS 10.15 or later, iOS 13 or later, or iPadOS 13 or later. Business Chat assists you with answering inquiries, resolving problems, getting shopping recommendations, using Apple Pay to make transactions, and more. **Note:** To differentiate Business Chat communications from iMessage messages (which display in blue text bubbles) and SMS or MMS messages (which appear in green text bubbles), your messages will appear in dark gray text bubbles when you send them.

- Use Maps to find the company you wish to speak with on your Mac or open an email from the company.
- Click **a link in the email or the Message button on the Map Info screen** to initiate a conversation. If this is your first message to this company, a fresh dialogue will start. If not, you are free to carry on with your discussion.
- In the message field located at the window's bottom, type your message and hit **Return**. The types of content that you can include are the same as those that you can send messages to groups or individuals.

You might be required to choose an answer from a list during a business chat (e.g., picking a time for an appointment or from a list of options for products). Delete the conversation to cease getting messages from a business chat. As an alternative, you can disable alerts.

Stop receiving messages on your Mac

You can log out of iMessage if you would like to stop seeing messages on your Mac.

- Select **Messages > Settings, click iMessage, and then click Settings** from within the Messages app on your Mac.
- After you click **Sign Out**, make sure you want to sign out. You stop receiving messages on your Mac when you log out of iMessage.

Note: You can choose to no longer receive messages at your phone number by unselecting the number that appears below under "You can be reached for messages at."

Setting Up and Making FaceTime Calls

Using an Apple device, FaceTime video calls allow users to see and speak with one another. The Wi-Fi connection on your Mac is used for FaceTime video conversations.

Make a FaceTime video call

- Click **New FaceTime in the Mac FaceTime app.**
- Enter the person you wish to call, phone number, or email address in the New FaceTime window. You might have to hit Return. You can enter the person's name or choose them

from Suggested if they are already in your Contacts. Additionally, contacts from the New FaceTime window can be added.

- Either utilize **the Touch Bar or click FaceTime.**

Answer a FaceTime video call

Even when FaceTime is closed, you can still take calls provided you're logged in and have FaceTime enabled. **When a notification shows in the upper-right corner of the screen on your Mac, choose one of the following actions:**

- Click **Accept** to answer an incoming call.
- Receive a video call just like any other call: Select **Answer as Audio** after clicking the down arrow next to Accept. The camera turns off automatically when you're on a phone call or audio call.
- Take a call, and then end the one you're on: Select **"End & Accept."**
- Click **Decline** to end a call.

To send a text message or set a reminder, you may additionally select the down arrow next to Decline.

Decline a FaceTime video call

Even when FaceTime is closed, you can reject calls provided you are logged in and have FaceTime enabled. **When a notification shows in the upper-right corner of the screen on your Mac, choose one of the following actions:**

- **Decline a call**: Select **Decline**. The person calling notices that you're not in the office. Advice: You can block the caller if it was made by someone you don't want to hear from again.
- **Refuse a call and use iMessage to deliver a message**: Select **Reply with reply from the drop-down menu by clicking the arrow next to Decline,** enter your reply, and hit Send. The caller and you both need to be logged into iMessage.
- **Turn down a call and make a note to call back later:** To set the time for when you wish to get a reminder, click **the down arrow next to Decline.** When the time comes, a notification appears on your screen. Click **it to view the reminder, and click the link to initiate the call.**

End a FaceTime video call

- Move the cursor over the call window and select the **"Leave Call" button (or use the Touch Bar) to end the call.**

Start a new Group FaceTime call

- Click **New FaceTime in the Mac FaceTime app.**
- To add callers to the New FaceTime window, you **must input the caller's phone number or email address. You might have to hit Return.** You can choose to select the individual from Suggested or enter their name if they are saved in your Contacts.
- Click **FaceTime to initiate the Group FaceTime call**, or use the **Touch Bar or the down arrow to select FaceTime Audio.** You can select between making a phone call or a FaceTime audio call if you select FaceTime Audio and your Mac is configured to make calls. The camera turns off automatically when you're on a phone call or audio call.

Add more people to a FaceTime video call

If the participants' Apple devices fulfil the required specifications, you can invite other individuals to participate in a FaceTime or Group FaceTime video conversation. You can share a FaceTime link with individuals who are using an Android or Windows smartphone, allowing them to participate in the online call.

- Click the **Sidebar button in the menu bar when on a FaceTime or Group FaceTime video conference on your Mac, and then select Add People.**

- In Contacts, type a person's name, phone number, or email address. (You might have to hit **Return.**) Additionally, you can choose a person from Suggested. In the To field, type the contact details for each person you want to add at once.
- Press **Add.**

Click **Sidebar, and then Ring to send an alert to a caller who hasn't joined the call yet.** The screen displays each participant's picture or initials as a tile. The title of the person on the call advances to the front and becomes more noticeable when they speak or when you click on it.

Integrating FaceTime with Other Devices

With your iPhone, you can initiate a FaceTime call and transfer it to another device that is logged in with the same Apple ID. You may utilize your iPhone as a webcam and microphone for FaceTime calls on your Mac or Apple TV by utilizing Continuity Camera and Mic. It should be noted that the contact details you have chosen for the call, as displayed in **Settings > FaceTime,** must correspond with the contact details you have chosen on the device you wish to transfer control of.

Hand off a FaceTime call from iPhone to iPad or Mac

You can transfer a FaceTime call from your iPhone to your iPad or Mac. Your devices must be running macOS 13, iOS 16, or iPadOS 16 or later to transfer a FaceTime call. On both devices, you need to be logged in using the same Apple ID.

- While on a FaceTime conversation on your iPhone, take one of the following actions on the other device:
    - Press the alert containing the recommendation to "Move call to this [device]."
    - On the top of the screen, tap the **Video Handoff button**. A call preview displaying your audio, video, and microphone options is displayed.
- Ensure that the settings are correct, and then hit Switch or Join. The call switches to the new device. On the originating device, a banner shows verifying that the call was resumed elsewhere, as well as a Switch button that you can use to resume the call.

Hand off a FaceTime call from your iPhone to Apple TV 4K

When signed in with the same Apple ID on both devices, you can initiate (or receive) a FaceTime call on your iPhone and then transfer it to the larger screen of Apple TV 4K (2nd generation and later). After you hand off the conversation, it continues on Apple TV, with your iPhone acting as a webcam and microphone for Apple TV during the call. Continuity Camera for Apple TV is accessible on iPhone XR, iPhone XS, and later models, as well as Apple TV 4K (2nd generation and later).

CHAPTER 8
PERSONAL ORGANIZATION

The MacBook Air M4 includes strong tools and features that help with personal organization, making it simpler to manage your work, schedule, notes, and documents. These features combine to make the MacBook Air M4 an amazing personal organizing tool, allowing you to efficiently and easily manage your time, projects, and information. Whether you're a student, a professional, or just seeking to stay organized, the MacBook Air M4 has everything you need to keep your life on track. In this chapter, you will learn about the many characteristics that you may apply to ensure that you have a fairly seamless organization.

Managing Apple ID and iCloud Settings

Your Apple ID grants you access to all Apple services, such as the App Store, Apple Music, iCloud, iMessage, FaceTime, and more. After logging in with your Apple ID, you may access Apple ID settings to modify your private data, sign-in and security preferences, payment and shipping information, and others.

- On your Mac, navigate to the **Apple menu -> System Settings**

And then select [your name] at the very top of the sidebar. If you don't see your name, select **"Sign in with your Apple ID,"** **input your Apple ID (or a different email or phone number on file), and then enter your password. If you don't already have an Apple ID, you can set up one.**

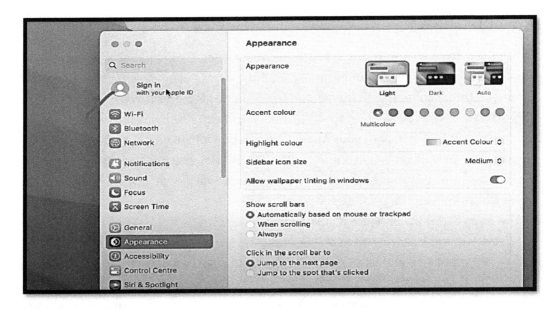

- **Choose any of the subsequent items to control the Apple ID configurations on your Mac:**
  - **Personal Information**: These options allow you to update the picture, name, and birthday linked with your Apple ID.
  - **Sign-In & Security**: These options allow you to update your Apple ID's contact information, password, authorized phone numbers, and security settings.
  - **Payment & shipment**: These choices allow you to view the payment method or alter the shipment address connected with your Apple ID.
  - **iCloud**: Use these settings to choose the iCloud capabilities you wish to use, control iCloud storage, and enable iCloud+ features.
  - **Media & Purchases**: These choices allow you to change your account settings, subscriptions, and download/purchase requirements.
  - **Family Sharing**: Create and administer a Family Sharing group to share your subscriptions, purchases, location, and other information with up to five family members.
  - **Devices**: Utilize this list to view and control the trusted gadgets that use your Apple ID.
  - **Contact Key Verification**: Utilize this option to ensure that you are only sharing messages with the intended recipients (macOS 14.2 or later).
  - **Sign out**. Sign out of your Apple ID.
  - **About Apple ID and Privacy**: Learn more about the Apple Privacy Policy, which protects your Apple ID information.

What is iCloud?

iCloud helps you store your most critical data, such as images, files, and backups, secure, up-to-date, and accessible from all of your devices. iCloud also allows you to easily share photographs, files, notes, and other content with friends and family. iCloud features a free email account and 5 GB of free data storage. You can upgrade to iCloud+ to get extra storage and features.

- To get started, **log in with your Apple ID and set up iCloud on your Mac**. When you sign in, important iCloud capabilities such as iCloud Photos and iCloud Drive are instantly enabled. You can enable or disable these functionalities at any moment, as well as personalize the settings for each device.

Follow the steps below to configure iCloud on your Mac;

- **Get any of the following done on your Mac;**
  - **macOS 13 and later**: Select **Apple menu > System Settings,** [your name] at the top of the sidebar, and then iCloud. If you don't see your name, click **"Sign in with your Apple ID," input your Apple ID (or a different email or phone number on file), input your password, and then select iCloud.**
  - **macOS 12 and earlier**: Select **Apple menu -> System Preferences, then Apple ID, and finally iCloud.** If you do not see Apple ID, click **Sign In, input your Apple ID and password, and then select iCloud.**
- Switch on or choose each application or feature.

To make use of iCloud on your Mac, follow the steps below;

iCloud feature	Description
Photos and videos	All of your photographs and videos. Always available. iCloud images securely store your images and videos, and you can access them from any device or on the web at iCloud.com. Shared Albums makes it simple to share photographs and videos with those who you choose and invite them to contribute photos, videos, and notes to your shared albums. With iCloud Shared Photo Library, you can work with up to five family members or friends to create a shared collection of photographs and videos, allowing you to enjoy more complete memories in one place.
iCloud Drive	Store all your files safely in iCloud Drive. iCloud Drive securely stores and organizes your data. Access and update them across all of your gadgets and on iCloud.com. You can also add your Mac Desktop and

	Documents files to iCloud Drive, making them available from anywhere. You can share and collaborate on items saved in iCloud with others. You determine who can see your material and make changes. If participants make changes to the content, everyone may view them in real-time.
Family Sharing	Sharing music, books, apps, and subscriptions with your family. Family Sharing allows you and up to five other family members to share access to wonderful Apple services such as Apple Music, Apple TV+, iCloud+, Apple Fitness+, Apple News+, and Apple Arcade. Your group can additionally share purchases from iTunes, Apple Books, and the App Store, as well as an iCloud storage plan and a family photo album. You may even assist each other find missing devices. When you join iCloud+, you may share all of its features and included capacity with your family.
iCloud Private Relay	iCloud Private Relay. Conceal your IP address and browsing history in Safari, and protect your unencrypted web traffic so that no one, even Apple, can see who you are or what websites you visit. Available with iCloud Plus.
Hide my Email	Create unique, random email addresses that are forwarded to your inbox and can be erased at any time to protect your privacy. Available through iCloud+.
Favorite applications	Sync your email, calendars, notes, contacts, reminders, messages, and more across all of your devices.
Safari bookmarks, open tabs, Reading Lists, and Tab Groups	Sync your current browser tabs across all of your gadgets, visit the same bookmarks, and browse articles from your Reading List when offline. Plus, keep your Tab Groups up to date across all of your devices and communicate with others.

iCloud Keychain	iCloud allows you to securely store passwords, credit cards, and other data. Safari and other compatible web browsers will automatically fill in your information.
iCloud Storage	Everyone starts with 5 GB of free iCloud storage, which can be upgraded at any time. Your app and iTunes Store purchases do not count against your iCloud storage space, so you just need it for photographs, videos, files, and device backups. Data stored in iCloud is secured, and two-factor authentication ensures that your account can only be accessed from trusted devices.

iCloud+

iCloud+ has all of the functionality of iCloud, as well as premium extras like iCloud Private Relay, Hide My Email, HomeKit Secure Video compatibility, support for custom email domains, and unlimited data storage.

- **iCloud Private Relay**: Conceal your IP address and surfing activities in Safari to protect your unencrypted web traffic while maintaining browsing performance.
- **Hide My Email**: Using Hide My Email, you may generate unique, random email addresses that go to your inbox, allowing you to send and receive emails without sharing your email address.
- **HomeKit Secure Video**: Use the Home app to connect your home security cameras and record footage, which you can then access from anywhere while remaining private and secure.
- **Custom email domain**: With iCloud.com, you may buy a custom email domain or import one you currently have and use it with iCloud Mail.

Upgrade to iCloud+

Upgrade to iCloud+ for more storage and premium features such as iCloud Private Relay, a service that protects your online privacy; Hide My Email, a simple way to generate a unique, random email address whenever you need one; and expanded support for HomeKit Secure Video recording, allowing you to set up more security cameras.

- On your Mac, navigate to the **Apple menu -> System Settings, and then choose [your name] at the top of the sidebar.** If you don't see your name, click "Sign in with your Apple ID," then insert your Apple ID (or a Reachable At email address or phone number that you entered in your Apple ID settings), followed by your password. If you don't already have an Apple ID, you can set up one.

- On the right, **click iCloud, followed by Manage.**
- Choose **Change Storage Plan or Add Storage, and then choose one of the following**:
  - o **Upgrade**: Select the amount of storage you want, select Subscribe to iCloud+ or Next, and then follow the on-screen instructions.
  - o **Downgrade:** Choose Downgrade Options and then follow the on-screen instructions. The downgrade takes action after your current monthly or annual membership expires. If you drop to 5 GB of storage, you will lose access to iCloud+ services. If your iCloud storage surpasses your new storage plan capacity, iCloud will not sync or update your details until you raise your storage capacity or delete data to free up space.

Share iCloud+

Once you've configured Family Sharing, you can share your iCloud+ subscription with other members of your Family Sharing group. If you join a Family Sharing group that subscribes to iCloud+ or Apple One and already have a membership, your subscription is not renewed on your next payment date; instead, you use the subscription of the group. If you join a non-subscriber Family Sharing group, the group will use your subscription. To stop sharing iCloud+ with a Family Sharing group, cancel your subscription, leave the group, or stop using Family Sharing.

Using Calendar, Contacts, and Notes

Calendar

The Calendar software allows you to keep track of all your meetings, activities, and appointments in one spot.

Here is how to start:

Add multiple accounts

Calendar allows you to add numerous accounts and manage all your events in one location. Open the Calendar app, select **Calendar > Add Account, and then follow the on-screen directions.**

Create events

You can use events to plan meetings, appointments, and family activities, among other things. Choose the **Add Event icon in the upper-left side of the Calendar window, insert your event information, and press Return.**

Add information to events

After you've established an event, you can provide pertinent information such as notes, URLs, and attachments. Double-click the event, then select **Add Notes, Add URL, or Add Attachment. Enter the information you want to include.**

Set alerts

You can set notifications to remind yourself about future calendar events. Double-click the **event, then click the time and finally select an option from the Alert pop-up menu.**

Invite people to events in Calendar on Mac

You can invite individuals to participate in events utilizing their names or email addresses. You can also invite groups to events utilizing their names or email addresses (for example, members@example.org). To invite people or organizations by name or email address, they must be in your Contacts app or use the same service provider as your calendar account.

- Double-click or force-click the event in your Mac's Calendar program, then selects **Add Invitees or tap next to any existing invitations. (You can also choose an event and utilize the Touch Bar.)**
- Enter each invitee's name or email address, and then hit **Return**. When you enter a name or email address, Calendar searches your Contacts and Mail applications, as well as associated calendar servers, for a match. If you touch **Return** before Calendar finds a match or before you complete entering an email address, the invitee is not added. After you input two invitees, Calendar recommends the next invitee depending on your

previous contacts with them, such as who you have frequently or recently invited to the same meeting. A marker next to each invitee displays their status, such as whether they are available, busy, or have responded yes, no, or maybe.

- If you find Check Availability underneath the last invitee, click it to discover if they are free or busy. Check Availability appears only if your event is stored in a calendar provider that maintains availability, such as CalDAV. The Availability window displays invitees' free and busy times. To determine an event time with the least or no conflicts, you can:
  - Move the event: Drag the event block.
  - See another day by clicking the arrows at the top of the window.
  - See the following time all invitees are available. Click t**he next available time**.
- Choose **Send.** To eliminate an invitee, select them and then tap the Delete key. If you frequently invite the same people to events, you can make a list of them in the Contacts app. Then, when you insert the list's name, each person is invited to the event. If your calendar service provider supports group email addresses, you can add them as invitees, and all group members will be invited.

Contacts

View individual contacts as well as contact lists. In your Mac's Contacts software, do one or more of the following things:

- **See a contact**: Select one of the contacts from the list. Contact information is displayed on the right.

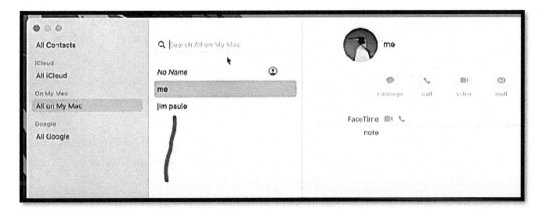

- View a contact in a separate window. **Click twice on a contact in the list, or choose it and then select Card > Open in Separate Window.**

You may rapidly browse for emails, messages, events, and files mentioning a specific contact. Control-click a contact in the list, then select the Spotlight command.

View lists of contacts

In your Mac's Contacts software, do any of these things:

- **See lists**: To display lists in the sidebar, select View > Show Lists.
- **View contacts in a list:** Choose **a list or Smart List from the sidebar.**
- **See which lists a contact belongs to**. Choose **a contact, then hit and press the Option key**. Lists containing the contact are marked in blue in the sidebar.
- **View all contacts**: Select **All Contacts from the sidebar.** This list combines contacts from many accounts.
- **View contacts in a network directory service**: Select the directory from the sidebar and then look for a contact.

Notes

Quick Notes: Quick Note allows you to scribble down ideas and add links regardless of what you're doing on your Mac. Your Quick Note remains visible on the screen while it is open, allowing you to quickly choose and add information from other apps. **If you're working in another program and want to jot something down, you may easily create a Quick Note. Do any of the following:**

- Use the keyboard shortcut: Press **and hold the Fn or Globe keys**, then press **Q.**
- Use hot corners: Place the pointer in the bottom-right corner of the screen (the default hot corner for Quick Note), and then choose **the note that appears.**

To close a Quick Note, select the red Close button in the top left corner of the note. To reopen the Quick Note, utilize any of the techniques listed above. To constantly begin a new Quick Note (rather than opening the old one), select **Notes > Settings, then uncheck "Always resume to last Quick Note."** Furthermore, with the use of Quick Notes, you can include content from Safari to QuickNote by following the set of instructions below;

- You can quickly highlight text on a website and add it immediately to a Quick Note.
- Open a webpage in Safari on your Mac, then pick the text you wish to save as a Quick Note.
- Control-click **the text, and then select New Quick Note or Add to Quick Notes. A link is displayed in the Quick Note, and the text in Safari is highlighted.** When you revisit the website, the text remains highlighted.

Search your notes in Mac

You may simply discover the note you want by searching for specific words, an emoji, or an attachment, or using a suggested search. **You can search for certain language or photos in your notes, narrow your search to a specific account, or search within a single note. Your search reveals relevant information in:**

- The body of every note
- The file names of links in your notes
- You've attached PDF files to your notes.
- Drawings you made on an iPhone, iPad, or iPod touch and attached to your notes.
- Handcrafted text in any notes.
- What is contained within the image you're looking for (for example, "bike")
- Text in a scanned file attached to a note.

In the Notes program on your Mac, perform one of the following.

- **Search for a certain account**: Click **a folder in the account you wish to search**, and then click **the magnifying glass to see the search field**. Next, click **the arrow (next to the magnifying glass) and select Current Account.**
- **Select the magnifying glass to open the search field**, then click t**he arrow (closest to the magnifying glass) and select All Accounts.**

Note: This step is only required if you have several accounts (such as iCloud and On My Mac).

- To narrow your search to only some of your notes, click the magnifying glass to see the search area, then select one of the suggested searches (such as Shared Notes or Notes with Attachments).
- Enter your search term and hit **Return**. Type what you're looking for in the same way you'd speak it (natural language search).

Below are some samples of natural language query phrases:

- Notes created last week.
- "modified today"
- "June from last year"
- "with documents about remodel"

All of the notes that fit your search query are presented, along with the folder in which they are stored. Top Hits, which appears first in the results, is a combination of notes that you've recently updated, those with the best match (maybe in the title), and other criteria. Even if your protected notes are unlocked, only the title is checked if you have locked a note. Search results include notes from the Recently Deleted folder.

Attach pictures, PDFs, and more in Notes on Mac

You can include additional files, PDFs, movies, and pictures with your notes. You can also connect map locations and webpage previews if you utilize upgraded iCloud notes or notes on your Mac. (You can add map locations or web page URLs, but you won't see previews for them if you haven't upgraded your iCloud notes or are working with an account that isn't connected to iCloud.) **You are not able to connect files, map locations, or webpage previews if your notes are stored in an Exchange account.**

- Choose a note in the notepad list or click twice on a note in the gallery view in the Mac Notes program. Attachments, tables, and links cannot be added to a locked note until it has been unlocked.
- To add an attachment, take any of the following actions:
  - You can add a file from the Finder or the desktop: In the note, **drag a file.**
  - Include a Mac file in the list: Click **Attach after choosing Edit > Attach File and choosing the file.**
  - You can add a picture to the note by dragging it straight from your Photos collection. Alternatively, select **Photos from the toolbar after clicking the Media button in Notes, and then drag a picture from the resulting window.**
  - Put a picture or scan from the camera on your iPhone or iPad here: To take a picture or scan a document with your iPhone or iPad and insert it into your note, click at the beginning of a line, select **File > Insert from iPhone or iPad, and then select Take Photo or Scan Documents**. (Needs iOS 12 or later, iPadOS 13 or later, and macOS 10.14 or later.)
  - Add a drawing from your iPad or iPhone: To make a drawing with your finger or an Apple Pencil on your iPad and insert it into a note, click at the beginning of a line, select **File > Insert from iPhone or iPad, and then select Add drawing**. (Requires iOS 13 or iPadOS 13 or later; macOS 10.15 or later is required.)

If you are viewing a note with attachments, select **View > Attachment View, then select Set All to Small or Set All to Large to adjust the size of all photos, scanned documents, or PDFs. Control-click an attachment, select View As, and then pick an option to adjust its size.** The appearance of huge drawings in notes cannot be altered.

Organizing Reminders and Tasks

Reminders

You may add reminders for tasks, to-do lists, and anything else you want to stay organized. To further structure your lists, use subtasks. All of your Apple devices that you have set up with the same accounts display your new reminders and modifications.

Note: When using updated iCloud reminders, all of the capabilities of Reminders covered in this guide are accessible. Using accounts from different providers prevents you from accessing some features.

- Choose **a reminder list from the sidebar of the Mac Reminders program**.
- In the upper-right corner, click the **Add button (or use the Touch Bar).**

- Give the reminder a title. A suggestion displays if the title you begin entering matches a previously finished reminder from the list; click it to swiftly enter the item again.
- **Take one of the following actions:**
  - **Include a note**: Below the text of the reminder, type a note. To make your notes simpler to read, utilize formatting options like bold or italicized text and bulleted lists (choose **Edit > Font or Edit > Bullets and Numbering**).
  - To set a time and date for a reminder, click **Add Date, select an existing date, or select Custom to utilize the calendar to select a date.** Once a date has been entered, you can optionally click **Add Time and select a recommended time. The reminder is active for the entire day if no time is entered.**
  - Remember this the next time you go somewhere or arrive at one: Select a suggested location by clicking Add Location, or type the name of a location and select from the list of options.
  - Remind yourself to tag things: Choose the **Tag button, select an existing tag, or choose New Tag to add a new tag.**
  - To mark a reminder, simply click the **Flag icon.**

Tasks

Exploring the Maps App

Directions for driving, walking, using public transit, and cycling are available. You can add more stops to your route when driving. For easy access while on the road, you may also email the directions to your iPhone, iPad, or Apple Watch.

Note: Not all nations or areas have directions for numerous stops.

- **Choose from the following actions in the Mac's Maps app:**
  - After selecting the **Directions button from the toolbar, input the beginning and destination locations.**
  - After selecting your location—such as a landmark or pin on a map—click the **Directions button on the place card.**
  - You can enter another place to begin, but Maps utilizes the one that is now displayed. To change the positions of your beginning and conclusion, you can also drag the **Reorder button next to the place.**
- Select **the option that says Drive, Walk, Transit, or Cycle.**
- To view the list of directions, choose the **Trip Details icon adjacent to a route. When driving, some possible directions are:**

Route planning for electric vehicles: Look for charging stations along the way and monitor your vehicle's current charge (if it fits).

Congestion zones: These areas serve to alleviate traffic in densely populated parts of large cities such as Singapore, London, and Paris. When these zones are in effect, you can find a route around them.

License plate restrictions: Depending on your eligibility, you can obtain a route through or around a restricted area in Chinese cities that restricts entry to populated areas.

- **Get any of the following done;**
  - Focus on a single step: In the list of instructions, click **the step.**
  - Select when you want to depart or arrive: Click **Plan to select when you want to leave or arrive if you're driving or using public transit.**
  - Choose the **Trip Details button** once more to close the directions list.

CHAPTER 9

CREATIVE AND PRODUCTIVITY TOOLS

Using iWork Suite: Pages, Numbers, and Keynote

Keynote, Pages, and Numbers are the finest tools for doing outstanding work. Starting is made simple with the use of design tools and templates. With an Apple Pencil, you can even annotate and add illustrations to your iPad. Additionally, your team may collaborate in real time whether they are using a PC, a Mac, an iPad, or an iPhone. For anyone seeking to produce papers, spreadsheets, and presentations of high caliber, the MacBook Air M4's iWork Suite is a fantastic option. **Below are the various things you would be able to achieve with the use of this suite;**

- Usability: The programs are made to be as simple as possible to use, even for novices, while also providing sophisticated functionality for more experienced users.

- Smooth connection: The iWork Suite offers a smooth experience across all of your Apple devices thanks to its strong connection to macOS and iCloud. This makes it simple to begin working on a project on your iPad or iPhone and finish it later on your MacBook Air.

- Collaboration Features: Working with people in the same office or on the other side of the world is made simple by the real-time collaboration capabilities. This is very helpful in the remote work world of today.

- Beautiful Design: The iWork Suite demonstrates Apple's well-known attention to design. Producing visually beautiful work is made simple by the tools and templates accessible, whether or not you're preparing a presentation, spreadsheet, or document.

- Frequent Updates: Apple adds new features and enhancements to the iWork Suite regularly. This guarantees that you will always be able to use the newest equipment and software.

Pages: Document Creation

- **Making and Editing Documents**: Pages is a feature-rich word processor that makes it simple to produce eye-catching documents. Pages have a large selection of templates and formatting tools that are useful whether you're writing a report, creating a flyer, or crafting a letter. Collaboration is facilitated by sophisticated features like change tracking and comments, while the user-friendly interface makes it simple to contribute text, photos, tables, and charts.

- **Collaboration and Communication**: Pages facilitate instantaneous collaboration, permitting numerous people to work on a document at once. Your document can be instantly shared via email, iCloud, or exported to other formats like Word, PDF, or ePub.

Pages are therefore perfect for usage in academic and professional contexts in addition to personal endeavors.

- **Design and Layout capabilities**: Pages provide sophisticated layout capabilities, such as exact alignment guidelines, drag-and-drop functionality, and customized templates. From straightforward text files to intricate brochures and newsletters, these capabilities make it simple to generate visually appealing documents.

Numbers: Spreadsheet Management

- **Data Organization and Analysis**: Apple's solution for managing spreadsheets is called Numbers, and it provides a more graphical interface than other spreadsheet programs. You can make interactive charts, arrange data into tables, and use built-in formulas to carry out intricate computations. You may freely arrange tables and charts on Numbers' flexible canvas, which makes it simple to create spreadsheets that are both aesthetically pleasing and useful.
- **Templates & Customization**: To get you started, Numbers includes several templates. These include project timelines, reports, and budgets as well as expenditure trackers. To make sure that your spreadsheets are customized to your unique needs, you may either make your own from the start or modify existing templates to fit your demands.
- **Real-Time Collaboration**: Numbers allow for real-time collaboration, just like Pages. Spreadsheets allow multiple people to work on them at once, and changes are shown instantly. Teams working on data-driven initiatives such as financial reports, budgets, or other related tasks may find this tool especially helpful.

Keynote: Presentation Creation

- **Creating Professional Presentation Designs**: Keynote is an effective tool for developing presentations that are visually striking. You can create visually appealing and educational presentations with a variety of themes, animations, and effects. With its user-friendly design tools and drag-and-drop capability, Keynote's UI is easy to use by users of all skill levels.
- **Animations and Transitions**: Creating dynamic animations and transitions is one of Keynote's best capabilities. A range of built-in effects make it simple to animate text, objects, and slides. For example, the "Magic Move" transition lets you make smooth, expert animations between presentations.
- **Presenting and Sharing:** There are several ways to present and distribute your work with Keynote. Presenting straight from your MacBook Air, streaming to an Apple TV via AirPlay, or exporting your presentation as PowerPoint, PDF, or video files are all possible options.

A timer, notes, and a sneak peek at the following slide are just a few of the extra tools the presenter display feature gives you to help you deliver your presentation with ease.

Exploring Creative Applications: Photos, iMovie, and Procreate

Photo

Mac Photos presents your finest images in an immersive, dynamic style. With the help of robust search capabilities, locate the images you're looking for. Sort your collection into albums, or use smart albums to automatically organize your photos. Utilize your preferred picture programs or the simple built-in editing tools to enhance your images and movies. Additionally, you can maintain all of your images and videos on your Mac, Apple TV, iPhone, iPad, and even PC up to date by using iCloud Photos.

Memories

Memories compile your greatest images and videos into an unforgettable film that you can share and customize, complete with title sequences, theme music, and dramatic transitions. If you have access to Apple Music, you can receive customized song recommendations. For you to relish a carefully chosen assortment of your travels, vacations, friends, family, dogs, and more. Additionally, any changes you make to a Memory when using iCloud Photos automatically sync to your other devices.

Get focused on your best shots

Photos highlight the greatest images in your collection while concealing screenshots, receipts, and duplicates. Organize your images by the date they were taken with the Days, Months, and Years views. Larger previews of your best photos draw attention to them, and Live Photos and movies instantly play to bring your library to life. In the Months and Years displays, photos also highlight significant events like birthdays, anniversaries, and travels.

Get your library filled and not your device

Making the most of the space on your Mac can be facilitated with iCloud Photos. All of your high-resolution images and movies are saved in iCloud in their original formats when you select "Optimize Mac Storage," with storage-saving copies being retained on your Mac as needed. To access more images and movies than ever before, you may also optimize the storage on your iPhone, iPad, and iPod touch. iCloud offers you 5GB of free storage, with the opportunity to upgrade to a 2TB plan when your collection fills up.

- **Make an edit and see it modified in your cloud**: When you edit a photo, mark a photo as a favorite, or add to an album on your Mac, iCloud Photos updates the version on your iPhone, iPad, and iCloud.com. Likewise, any modifications made to your iOS or iPadOS devices will seamlessly transfer to your Mac.
- **Have all your pictures on all your devices**: You can access your whole Mac photo and video library from any device with iCloud Photos. Your iPhone photos, slow-motion videos, and selfies are automatically added to iCloud Photos, where they can be viewed on your PC, Mac, iOS, and iPadOS devices, Apple TV, and iCloud.com. All of your iCloud Photos-capable devices display the images and movies that you import onto your Mac from your DSLR, GoPro, or drone. Additionally, exploring your library always feels comfortable because your collection is arranged consistently across all of your Apple devices.

Resize, crop, collage, zoom, warp, GIF and lots more

Pose exceptional images with an extensive collection of robust yet user-friendly photo-editing tools. Instantaneously alter pictures taken in portrait orientation by applying five distinct lighting effects of studio caliber. Select Enhance to instantly make your shot better. Next, apply a filter to change its appearance. Instead, even if you're a novice, you may edit swiftly and expertly by using Smart Sliders. Markup enables you to annotate your photographs with text, shapes, doodles, and signatures. Also, you may create entertaining, little video loops to share using Live Photos. Additionally, you can modify a photo with an app like Photoshop and save your modifications to your Photos library, or you can use third-party app extensions like Pixelmator.

- **Bring even more life to your Live Photos**: The Loop effect can be used to alter a live photo to create an endless looping video that you can watch over and over. To play the action both forward and backward, try using Bounce. Alternately, use Long Exposure to blur water or lengthen light trails for a stunning DSLR-like appearance. For every Live Photo, you may also choose a key photo, silence it, and trim it.

Bring Photos to your Mac from iCloud

To view your images across all of your devices, if you use iCloud, make sure that iCloud images are enabled on your Mac, iPhone, and iPad.

- Navigate to **Photos > Settings on your Mac, choose iCloud**

And then pick iCloud Photos.

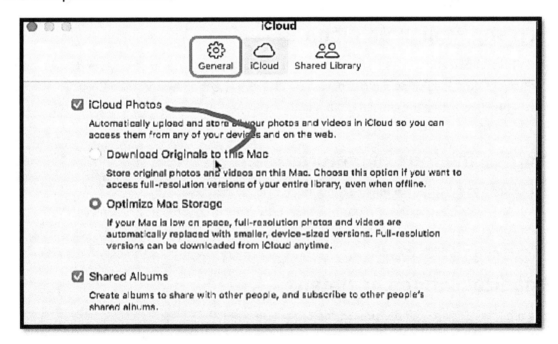

Browse your pictures

- Choose **Library in the sidebar**

Then select Years, Months, or Days from the toolbar to view your images by date of capture. Alternatively, click **All Images to view your entire collection.** Choose **People or Places in the** sidebar to view images of particular people or taken in particular places.

Crop and straighten pictures

Images taken at an angle can be straightened out by cropping them to remove undesired parts.

- After **double-clicking a picture**, select **Edit from the toolbar and then Crop.** To preserve the region, drag the chosen rectangle to encompass it. To change the angle of the picture, use **the Straighten slider.**

Improve the look of pictures

Easily change color, brighten images, and more.

- After **double-clicking a picture**, select **Edit from the toolbar.** To achieve the desired effect, click the arrow next to Light or Color and drag the slider, or **select Auto to let Photos handle it for you.**

Organize pictures in albums

Make albums to keep your pictures in the order you want.

- Select **File > New Album**, enters the album's name, then hit **Return.** Choose **Library in the** sidebar, and then drag images to the newly created album in the sidebar to add them to the album.

Create shared albums in Pictures on Mac

It's simple to make a shared album to share your pictures and videos once you enable shared albums.

Create a shared album

- Choose the pictures and videos you wish to share from the Photos program on your Mac.
- To create a new shared album, click the **Share icon in the toolbar, select Shared Albums, write a note if desired, and then click Share.**
- After entering the email addresses of the recipients of the shared album, give it a name. Make sure you use the email addresses that subscribers use to sign in with their Apple IDs if you want them to be able to access the shared album from an iPhone or iPad.
- Press the **Create button.** An email asking them to subscribe to your shared album is sent to the individuals you invite.

Viewed a shared album

- Select a **shared album from the list of shared albums in the sidebar of the Photos app on your Mac.** Alternatively, you can click twice **on a shared album to view it by selecting Shared Albums from the sidebar to view all of your shared albums in a window.**
- You may view all of your shared albums by clicking the **Back button.**

Stop sharing an album

To cease sharing an album with a particular person, take their name off the list of subscribers. You can remove a photo album if you want to completely cease sharing it. **WARNING:** A shared album that you remove will be instantly erased from both your devices and the devices of your subscribers. Before deleting the shared album, you should let your subscribers know if you think they would wish to save any images or videos from it. Additionally, confirm that you have downloaded any movies and pictures that you wish to preserve that other people have added to the album. Your Photos library retains the images you shared.

One of the following actions can be taken in the Mac's Photos app:

- Select a shared album from the sidebar, and then select **Delete Shared Album from the toolbar's Collaborate button.**
- To stop sharing an album, control-click on it and select **Delete Shared Album.**

IMovie

The newest Macs are known for their amazing power and low power consumption, which makes them perfect for creative work. Apple provides its users with free access to iMovie, one of the most widely used video editors on macOS. But to get the most out of it, you have to become acquainted with its features and user interface. I've broken down iMovie for Mac in this comprehensive section to get you started. First things first: you need to download iMovie to use it. On macOS Sonoma, it normally comes pre-installed. **However, if you've deleted it or are unable to locate it for any other reason, take the following actions:**

- Start **up the Mac App Store.**
- Select the search box located in the upper left corner.
- Select **iMovie.**
- Press the **Return key.**
- From the search result, pick the iMovie application.
- After selecting the **Get or Download option, watch for the installation to be completed.**

iMovie Basics

When iMovie is opened for the first time:

- Permit iMovie to access your collection of photos.
- To go through the welcome windows, click go.
- In the menu bar, select iMovie and then Settings (or Preferences for older macOS versions).
- Modify the configuration Go from that page if the defaults don't meet your needs.
- Projects and Media are the two primary categories on the home screen.
- You may view the photo and video library that is stored in the Photos app under Media.
- In regard to Projects, which is where we will concentrate. That is the start of the magic.

Using Trailers

As the name implies, the Trailers tool lets you use your movies to make Hollywood-style movie trailers. You can choose from more than twenty templates from different genres that Apple offers.

- Select **Create New from the Projects menu**.
- Select **Trailer.**
- Select **a template whose genre aligns with the mood you want to create**. You can watch a preview by clicking on the timestamp located beneath each template to see how long it is.
- When you're ready, select **Create from the drop-down menu in the lower right corner to open the editor.**

- The Storyboard, Shot List, and Outline are located in the lower portion of the screen.
  - You can complete the text details that will appear on your trailer, including the title, director, release date, and more, under the Outline area.
  - You have control over the images and videos you include in your project with Storyboard and Shot List.
- You can access My Media, where we are now working, as well as other sections, on the top bar.
- You can use Apple's sound effects or import music into the Audio area. But background music is already included in trailers; it's just there for extra audio editing.
- You can **select the title style for your trailer in the Titles section.**
- You can select t**he primary background for your project under Backgrounds.**
- With transitions, you can customize the animation's appearance when one video stops, and a new one begins.
- Select **Photos in the sidebar under My Media.**
- To add a video to the project, navigate **to the Videos folder.**
- To import a video, drag it to the **Project Media area in the sidebar once you've decided on one.**
- You can select a section of the imported video from the Storyboard and apply it to a specific area of the trailer.
- After that, you can continue to the following segment of the trailer. Complete them all, and never forget that you can use more films that you import from your photo gallery.
- With the tools that have been utilized thus far, carry on personalizing the trailer.
- Click the **Projects button** in the upper left corner of the screen when you're ready to export your project.
- After naming your project, click **OK.**
- You may then export your trailer from the Projects screen and share it with other applications or services.

Using Movies in iMovie

- For more ambitious projects, the Movies section offers more advanced video editing options.
- Click **Start New in the Projects screen**, then select Movie to start a movie project.
- It has a layout that looks a lot like the Trailer editor, especially in the upper left corner.
- Just as with trailers, import videos from your photo library and place them into the bottom portion.
- Continue **adding all of the videos that you choose to feature in your film.**

Music Production and Video Editing Essentials

Both novices and experts can now produce music and edit videos thanks to the MacBook Air M4, a strong, portable, and adaptable device. The MacBook Air M4, with its cutting-edge M4 chip, gorgeous Retina display, and smooth macOS integration, is a powerful tool for creative work. More information about the requirements for using the MacBook Air M4 for video editing and music production, including the tools, methods, and best practices, is provided below.

Music Production Essentials

- **Digital Audio Workstation**: With its ability to run strong DAWs like Logic Pro X, Ableton Live, and GarageBand, the MacBook Air M4 excels in the realm of music production. Specifically designed for macOS, Logic Pro X provides an extensive toolkit for music production, editing, and mixing. Smooth performance is guaranteed by the M4 chip, even when using sophisticated plugins and many tracks.

- **MDI Controllers and Audio Interfaces**: With the MacBook Air M4's Thunderbolt/USB 4 connectors, connecting MIDI controllers such as the Akai MPK Mini or Novation Launchpad is a simple process. By giving you direct control over your DAW, these controllers make it simpler to enter notes, start samples, and change settings. An audio interface like the Focusrite Scarlett 2i2 offers excellent input and output with little latency and crystal-clear sound quality for recording vocals or instruments.

- **Monitors and Headphones**: While producing music, precise monitoring is essential. Because the MacBook Air M4 has high-resolution audio output, it can be used with headphones like the Beyerdynamic DT 770 Pro or studio monitors like the Yamaha HS5. Because of the flat frequency response that these devices offer, you can precisely alter your mix.

- **Optimizing macOS for Music Production**: You may optimize macOS on the MacBook Air M4 for making music by configuring the system preferences to give performance priority. A few strategies to guarantee seamless operation include turning off pointless background activities, putting the power mode on high performance, and storing project data on an external SSD.

Video Editing

- **Video Editing Software**: The MacBook Air is capable of running industry-standard video editing programs like DaVinci Resolve, Adobe Premiere Pro, and Final Cut Pro X thanks to its potent M4 CPU. With its extensive effects capabilities, real-time editing, and sophisticated color grading, Final Cut Pro X is especially well-suited for macOS. Because of the MacBook Air M4's Retina display, you can edit with accuracy and see every detail in your video.

- **4K and HDR Editing**: The MacBook Air M4 can easily handle editing 4K and HDR footage. Smooth playing and quick rendering times are provided by the integrated GPU in the M4 processor, even when working with high-resolution video. Accurate color representation is made possible by the Retina display's P3 broad color gamut, which is necessary for editing at the professional level.
- **Graphics and Visual Effects**: With the use of programs like Motion and After Effects, the MacBook Air M4 can produce sophisticated visuals and visual effects. You may enhance your video projects by adding motion graphics, animations, and special effects with these tools. The M4 chip makes sure that there is no latency or crashes throughout these procedures.

CHAPTER 10
ENTERTAINMENT

The MacBook Air M4 is a fantastic gadget for enjoyment as well as a potent tool for work. This amazing gadget has an immersive audio system, a gorgeous Retina display, and cutting-edge electronics that provide an immersive multimedia experience. The MacBook Air M4 is an all-around entertainment center that can handle a variety of tasks, including gaming, content creation, streaming movies and music, and more. Its robust hardware and macOS's smooth service integration make it the perfect option for anyone seeking an all-encompassing entertainment experience. Regardless of your level of experience, the MacBook Air M4 provides all the features and tools you need to turn your leisure time into a productive and pleasurable experience.

Managing Music with the Music App

You may add songs, albums, playlists, and music videos from Apple Music to your music library as soon as you subscribe to the service. Your music library is available anytime you're signed in to Apple Music on your Mac, iPhone, iPad, iPod touch, Apple TV, or Android device. You can download music to your computer or device to listen to it whenever you want, even when you're not online, after adding it to your music library. Note: Not all nations or areas have access to Dolby Atmos, lossless, or Apple Music.

Add music to your Library

- **Try any of these suggestions to locate the music you want to add to the Mac's Music app:**
  - **See the suggestions that are personalized for you**: Find music you've recently played, custom playlists made just for you, genres you might enjoy, and more by clicking Home on the sidebar.
  - **Check out what's fresh on Apple Music**: Discover music by mood, new releases, charts, and more by **clicking the Browse button in the sidebar.**
- **One of the following can be done to add songs to your music library:**
  - Click the **Add button** after moving the pointer over an item.
  - Point the cursor on an object (such as a song or album), select **Add to Library from the More menu**, and then click **OK.**
  - The item can be dragged to the sidebar.
  - You can add a song, for instance, to a playlist or the library by dragging it.

o The songs in an Apple Music playlist that you add to your library are updated anytime the playlist owner updates them, but the individual songs are not displayed in your list of songs.

If these options aren't visible to you, there are three possible reasons: either you haven't joined Apple Music or you aren't logged in with your Apple ID, or the Sync Library option isn't checked in the Music settings: Select **Sync Library** by choosing **Music > Settings, click General, and then clicking OK.**

Download music to your computer

- Click **any option in the sidebar below the Library in the Mac's Music program**. Click **Songs, for instance, to see every song in your library.**
- Drag the pointer over an item in your music library to start downloading it to your computer. You can then choose to:
  - Press the "**Download**" button.
  - Select **Download after clicking the More option.**

The Dolby button will show up next to the item if the music you're downloading is compatible with Dolby Atmos, and you may choose to download it in stereo or Dolby Atmos. When available, pick **Songs > Settings, click General, and then check the box labeled "Download Dolby Atmos" to download songs in Dolby Atmos.** Please take note that the music you download to your computer via Apple Music cannot be manually transferred to an iPhone, iPad, or iPod, nor can it be burned to a disk. Only Apple Music allows users to download music straight to their devices.

Setting up Home Sharing

You must first configure Home Sharing on your Mac before using it.
- Select System Preferences from the Apple menu, and then click **General in the sidebar.**
- **On the right, select Sharing.**
- Activate Media Sharing, then **select Info**. There is no alt for the image next to it.
- Choose Home Sharing, then click **Turn On Home Sharing** after entering your Apple ID. For each computer or device connected to your home-sharing network, use the same Apple ID.

Using Home Sharing

Using Home Sharing on your Mac or PC, you can view shared libraries from other computers that are signed in with the same Apple ID and connected to the same Wi-Fi network. You must be logged in with the same Apple ID as the computer and linked to the same Wi-Fi network to view a shared library from a computer on your iPhone, iPad, iPod touch, or Apple TV.

Computers connected to the same Wi-Fi network can access your media library via Home Sharing. Additionally, you can stream TV series, movies, and music between computers that are approved. Verify that your computers are turned on, and awake and that iTunes or the Music app is open on Windows.

Using home sharing on your Mac; To use your media collection, go to:

- Launch **the Music application.**
- Use your Apple ID to log in if you're not already. For each computer or device connected to your home-sharing network, use the same Apple ID.
- Click **Library in the sidebar.**
- To access the media library, **click it.**

On your Apple TV, you may also browse images taken with your PC. Using a Mac: Select **System Preferences from the Apple menu**, and then click **General** in the sidebar. On the right, select Sharing. Choose **the Info button alt** supplied for Image placed **next to it after turning on Media Sharing.** Next, choose **to Share Pictures with Apple TV.**

Enjoying Podcasts, TV Shows, and Books

Podcasts

Listen to podcasts on Mac

You can play the entire podcast or just certain episodes when you find one you want to listen to.

- On your Mac, choose **any item in the sidebar of the Podcasts app.**
- Click the **Play button after dragging the pointer over the program or episode you want to watch.** The show art and playback controls appear at the highest point of the podcast window when the episode starts playing. Certain shows have original artwork that is displayed on the episode page and in the player for each episode.
- **Utilize the playback controls for any of the following actions:**
  - Press the Play or Pause button located in the center or utilize the Touch Bar's playback controls.
  - Moreover, you may play, pause, and continue an episode by using the Spacebar.
  - To advance or rewind an episode, click the **Skip Forward or Backward buttons, which will advance the playback in 30-second intervals. Alternatively, you can use the Touch Bar's playback controls.**
  - Rewind or fast-forward: Drag the progress handle to the left to rewind or to the right to fast-forward or select a point on the progress bar to jump straight to that spot. (Alternatively, you can utilize t**he Touch Bar's playback controls.)**

- o Modify the speed of the playback: After selecting **Controls > Playback Speed, select a speed.**
- o To change the volume, drag **the volume slider to the right or left (or use the Touch Bar's playback controls).**
- o Handle the episode (copying the URL, sharing the episode, or visiting the Show page, for instance): Move the cursor over the currently playing episode, select an option, and then click the **More button.**
- o Examine the description of the episode: Press **the "Episode Notes" icon**. Until you choose the **Episode Notes button once more to close it,** the episode description remains visible on the screen.

TV Shows

When it comes to enjoying Friday Night Baseball, MLS Season Pass, and other content on your Mac, the Apple TV app is the first place you should go. One location for all of your movies, TV series, MLS events, and more. MacOS Big Sur 11.0, macOS Monterey 12.0, and macOS Catalina 10.15, or later are required to use the Apple TV app. Friday Night Baseball and the MLS Season Pass require macOS Ventura 13.2 or later.

- • On your Mac, open **the Apple TV app.**
- • Use your Apple ID to log in if prompted and access your current membership or begin a free trial.
- • **Choose from any of the following sidebar categories or items:**
  - o Search for TV series and movies by title, cast, or crew.
  - o **Home**: Begin viewing movies, TV shows, and sports in one location. Utilize the Up Next row to locate items you've added or stuff you've begun but haven't completed.
  - o **Apple TV+**: Explore and watch Apple TV+, a subscription streaming service that includes Apple Originals (award-winning films, series, riveting dramas, innovative documentaries, kids' entertainment, comedies, Friday Night Baseball, and more), with new content added monthly.
  - o **MLS Season Pass:** Watch every Major League Soccer match, Audi MLS Cup Playoffs, and Leagues Cup in one spot, with consistent game timings and no blackouts.
  - o Use this all-in-one location to browse, buy, and rent the world's top movies and TV shows.
  - o **Channels:** Choose a channel that you've recently subscribed to.
  - o **Library**: View what you bought and rented, categorized by category.

Books

You can begin reading and enjoying the books once you receive them from the bookstore or download books that you have already purchased on other devices. You could like audiobooks if you'd rather have a book read aloud to you.

Open and move around in a book

- Double-click **a book to open it in the Books app on your Mac by selecting Books (or another collection) from the sidebar.** Note: Double-clicking the book will download it from iCloud if it has an iCloud status icon beneath it (you may need to log in first).

- **Navigate through the book;**
  - Refer to the contents table: Point the cursor to the top of the book, then, depending on the book, click either **the Thumbnails or the Table of Contents button.**
  - Navigate to the previous or next page: To select the arrow that appears, move **the pointer to the left or right edge of the book.** You can also utilize the Touch Bar, the keyboard's arrow keys, or swipe left or right across a trackpad or Magic Mouse.
  - Navigate to the top of the book, click **the magnifying glass**, then type a word, phrase, or page number to start a search. Another option is to pick some text, Control-click it, and select **Search.**

o **View the page you were just on**: After making a multipage jump, click the Back icon in the lower-left corner of the page. When browsing search results or different portions of the book's table of contents, this is helpful. Click the **Return icon in the bottom-right corner of the page to go back to the page you were on before.**

See what you are currently reading

On your Mac, select Home from the sidebar of the Books app. The books you are reading right now are listed in Continue. To view a list of books you've bought,

- Click **All in the sidebar under Library if you haven't begun reading any yet.**

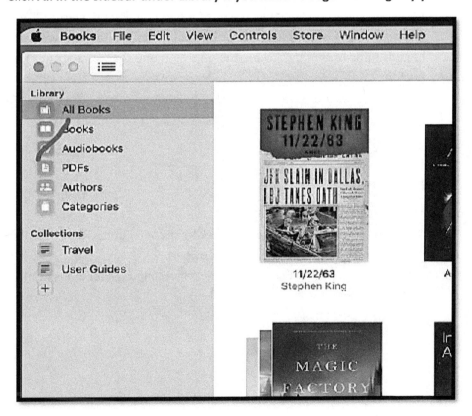

Drag the pointer over the title of a book or audiobook in Home, select **Remove from the menu, and then make your selection.**

Save your place with a bookmark

- Double-click a book to open it in the Books app on your Mac by selecting Books (or another collection) from the sidebar.

- Place the pointer at the top of the page you wish to bookmark, and then press the Bookmark icon (or use the Touch Bar). The Bookmark icon is solid if you already have a bookmark on the page.

Select the **Show Bookmarks button** to view every bookmark in the book. To delete a bookmark, select it by clicking **the Bookmark icon.**

Have a book read to you

- Double-click a book to open it in the Books app on your Mac by selecting Books (or another collection) from the sidebar.
- **Take one of the subsequent actions:**
  - When reading a book that has the Read Aloud function enabled, utilize the **Touch Bar or the Play button located in the toolbar at the top of the book.** Select a **page-turning option by clicking the pop-up menu that appears next to the Play button.**
  - Regarding any book: Navigate to the desired page and select **Edit > Speech > Begin Speaking.**

Translate text in a book

Choose the text you wish

- To translate in the MacBook app.
- Select **Translate [selection] by controlling-clicking the selection. (This content cannot be translated into Books if you do not see this option.)**
- After selecting the source language, select **the target language for translation.**

CHAPTER 11
NETWORKING AND SECURITY

For those who value strong networking and security capabilities, the MacBook Air M4 is a dependable option. It is a smart gadget that excels in both performance and security. The MacBook Air M4 is a great option for both personal and business use since it combines strong security features with powerful networking capabilities. It improves network performance and privacy with its support for the most recent Wi-Fi standards, smooth Bluetooth connectivity, and VPN choices. Complete data and privacy protection is offered by security features including Gatekeeper, two-factor authentication, and FileVault encryption. Through comprehension and application of these networking and security instruments, you can guarantee that your MacBook Air M4 continues to be a reliable and safe partner for all your technological endeavors.

Using AirDrop

You can wirelessly transfer files, images, movies, webpages, map locations, and more to a Mac, iPhone, iPad, or Apple Vision Pro that is close by using AirDrop.

- Click the **Share option after opening the file you wish to transmit**. The app window's image has no alt provided. You may also Control-click a file in the Finder and select Share from the shortcut menu.
- From the list of sharing choices, select AirDrop.
- **Select a receiver using the AirDrop sheet:**
  - Alternatively, launch the AirDrop window and drag files to the recipient:
  - In the Finder window's sidebar, choose **AirDrop.** Or use the menu bar to select **Go > AirDrop.**
  - Nearby AirDrop users are displayed in the AirDrop window. To the recipient displayed in the window, drag one or more documents, images, or other assets.

Connecting to Network Printers and Shared Devices

You must add a printer to your list of printers using the Printers & Scanners settings before you can use it. (If you moved from a Windows computer to a Mac, you can use the Printers & Scanners settings similarly to how you would use the Windows Printing control panel.) When a printer is added, macOS often connects to it via AirPrint. Install the most recent printing software from the manufacturer's website or the package that came with the printer, if needed.

Add a USB printer

All you need to do to connect a USB printer to your Mac is to update the printer's software. Install the most recent printing software from the manufacturer's website or the package that came with the printer, if needed.

- **Update the printer software on your Mac**: To find out if any updates are available for your printer model, contact the manufacturer of your printer.
- **Get your printer ready:** To unpack the printer, install the ink or toner, and add paper, follow the instructions that come with the device. Make sure that the printer is not displaying any problems after turning it on.
- **Establish a printer connection**: Attach the USB cord to the Mac. Make sure to download and install any new software that appears on-screen prompts.

Add a Wi-Fi or network printer

The printer may be available to you without any configuration if your Mac and printer are already linked to the same wireless network. Select File > Print, click the Printer pop-up menu, select Printers & Scanners settings or Nearby Printers, and then select your printer to verify. You can add your printer if you can't see it.

- **Update the printer software on your Mac**: To find out if any updates are available for your printer model, contact the manufacturer of your printer. You don't need to look for software upgrades if your printer is AirPrint compatible.
- **Get your printer ready:** To unpack the printer, install the ink or toner, and add paper, follow the instructions that come with the device. Make sure that the printer is not displaying any problems after turning it on.
- **Connect your printer:** To connect your printer to the network, follow the directions that come with it. To set up Wi-Fi printing, you may need to use a USB cable to connect your Wi-Fi printer to your Mac. Install the Mac software that was included with the printer after connecting it to your Mac, and then use the printer's setup aid to link it to your Wi-Fi network. The printer should stay connected to the Wi-Fi network even after you unplug the cables from your Mac and printer after setup.
- **Include the printer in your inventory of accessible printers**: Select **System Preferences from the Apple menu then select Printers & Scanners from the sidebar. (You might have to scroll below.)**

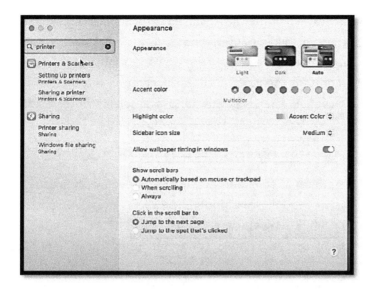

- Choose the **Add Printer, Scanner, or Fax option on the right if your printer isn't visible on the left.** A dialog box displaying the local network printers shows up.

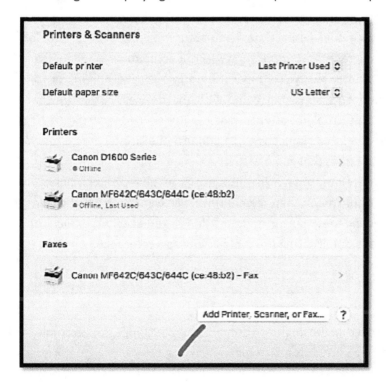

- Choose your printer from the list when it shows up, and then click **Add**. Your printer might not show up for a minute or two. Ensure to download and install any new software that appears on-screen prompts.

MacOS can typically identify if a printer has installed extra accessories like memory, duplex units, or extra paper trays when you add a printer. If not, a dialog box allowing you to specify them will show up. To fully utilize the installed accessories on your printer, make sure the settings in that dialog appropriately represent them. Print Center, located in the Utilities folder, allows you to easily add a printer. To configure a new printer for usage, select **Printer > Add Printer when Print Center is open**.

Add a network printer by indicating its IP address

You can add a network printer as an IP printer if the printer you wish to use isn't listed among the available printers. One of the following printing protocols must be supported by the printer: Internet Printing Protocol (IPP), HP Jetdirect (Socket), Line Printer Daemon (LPD), or AirPrint.

Note: The functioning of certain printers connected using these generic protocols may be restricted.

The printing protocol, model number, printer software name, and IP address or hostname of the network printer must all be known. You must also be aware of the name of any special queues it may be using. For assistance, see the person in charge of the server or printer.

- **Update the printer software on your Mac**: To find out if any updates are available for your printer model, contact the manufacturer of your printer. You don't need to look for software upgrades if your printer is AirPrint compatible.
- **Get your printer ready**: To unpack the printer, install the ink or toner, and add paper, follow the instructions that come with the device. Make sure that the printer is not displaying any problems after turning it on.
- **Establish a printer connection:** To connect the printer to the network, adhere to the setup instructions that came with it.
- Include the printer in your inventory of accessible printers: Select **System Preferences from the Apple menu then select Printers & Scanners from the sidebar.**
- After selecting the IP button and the **Add Printer, Scanner, or Fax icon on the right, enter the printer's details using the table below as a reference.**

Option	Description
Address	Input the hostname (printer.example.com, for example) or IP address (192.168.20.11, for example).
Protocol	**Select a printing protocol that works with your printer:**

	AirPrint: If the particular printer you're using supports it, you can use the AirPrint protocol to make printing and scanning choices available across Wi-Fi, USB, and Ethernet networks. To utilize printers that support AirPrint, you do not need to download or install any printer software. The AirPrint protocol is compatible with a large range of printers, including those made by Brother, Canon, Epson, Fuji, Hewlett Packard, Samsung, Xerox, and many more. Use the HP Jetdirect-Socket protocol to connect to a variety of printer manufacturers, including Hewlett-Packard. Accessibility to some older printers and print servers that employ this protocol is made possible by the Line Printer Daemon, or LPD. Modern printers and print servers can be accessed over the Internet Printing Protocol or IPP.
Queue	Enter your printer's queue name here. Try leaving the queue name blank or get in touch with your network administrator if you are unsure of it.
Name	Give the printer a meaningful name (such as Color Laser Printer) so that you can recognize it in the Printer pop-up menu.
Location	Note the printer's position (for instance, "outside my office") so that the Printer pop-up menu will recognize it.
Use	Present the printer's compatible software. Choose Select Software and choose your printer from the Printer Software list if you can't find the software you need. Try downloading and installing the printer software—also known as a printer driver—from the printer manufacturer if it isn't included in the Printer Software list. Depending on the kind of printer you have, you can also try selecting PCL or generic postscript printer software from the pop-up option.

Add a Bluetooth printer

You can print remotely to a Bluetooth-enabled printer if your Mac has Bluetooth® built-in, or if you're using a USB Bluetooth adapter.

- **Update the printer software on your Mac**: To find out if any updates are available for your printer model, contact the manufacturer of your printer. You don't need to look for software upgrades if your printer is AirPrint compatible.

- **Get your printer ready**: To unpack the printer, install the ink or toner, and add paper, follow the instructions that come with the device. Make sure that the printer is not displaying any problems after turning it on.
- **Establish a printer connection**: To ensure that your printer is prepared for a Bluetooth connection, refer to the instructions that come with it.
- **To your printer list, add your Bluetooth printer**: Select **System Preferences from the Apple menu, then select Printers & Scanners from the sidebar. (You might have to scroll below.)**
- On the right, select **the Add Printer, Scanner, or Fax button. Next, select the Default button.**
- Click Add after selecting the printer from the list of printers. Enter the name of the printer you expect to see in the search field and hit Return if it's not in the list.

Ensure that you have the most recent printer Bluetooth driver installed if your printer isn't listed. To obtain the most recent driver, contact the manufacturer. If you see a notification after connecting your printer asking you to download new software, please download and install it.

Add a Wi-Fi or mobile printer that needs a configuration profile

Installing a configuration profile may be necessary for some network printers for AirPrint to find the printer on your network. **Install the printer profile on your Mac by downloading or copying it, if one is given.**

- Double-clicking **the profile will open it on your Mac.**
- Click **Continue** when a window asking if you wish to install the profile appears.
- Click Install when a prompt asks you to confirm that you wish to install the profile. The profile is installed under the Privacy & Security settings' Profiles section. The printer can then be included in your printer list.
- Select **Apple menu > System Settings, then click Printers & Scanners in the sidebar to add your printer to the printer list.** (You might have to scroll below.)
- On the right, select the Add Printer, Scanner, or Fax button. Next, select the **Default button.**
- Click **Add after selecting the printer (seen in the Printers list as an AirPrint Profile)**. Make sure you have the most recent printer profile installed and that your computer can access the printer via a network path if your printer isn't showing up in the list. Ask your network administrator for the most recent version of the profile.

Configuring Security Settings: Firewall and Privacy

Use the Privacy & Security settings on your Mac to secure your encrypted data and control what information is visible to other users over the network or the internet. To modify these preferences, select **System Preferences from the Apple menu, then select Privacy & Security from the sidebar. (You might have to scroll below.)**

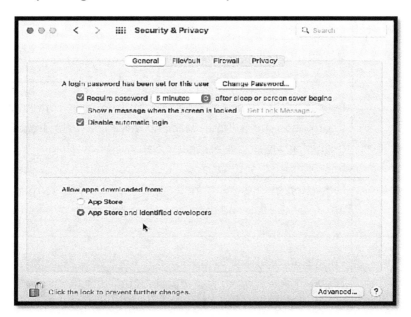

Option	Description
Location services	Give applications, system services, and websites permission to collect and utilize location-based data to offer a range of location-based services based on your Mac's present location. Click the Details button located at the bottom of the list on the right to view the exact system services that utilize your location. Turn on Location-Based Suggestions to give Siri and Safari suggestions permission to utilize your Mac's location.
Contacts	Permit apps to view your contacts. Access has been requested by the mentioned apps.

Reminders	Permit apps to view your reminders. Access has been requested by the mentioned apps.
Photos	Give apps access to your pictures. Access has been requested by the mentioned apps. **Note:** Other apps may still be able to access items that you have stored other than in the Photos Library.
Full disk access	Permit applications to access all files on your computer, including information from Time Machine backups, data from other apps (including Mail, Messages, Safari, and Home), and certain administrative settings for all users on this Mac. Access has been requested by the mentioned apps. Click the Add button, choose the app from the list, and then click Open to add it.
Input monitoring	Permit applications to track input from your trackpad, mouse, and keyboard even when you're using other programs. Access has been requested by the mentioned apps. Click the Add button, choose the app from the list, and then click Open to add it.
Sensitive content warning	Refrain from viewing images and videos that might be sensitive. Private images and videos seem hazy. You have the option to see them without any blur.
Apple advertising	Ads in Apple News, Stocks, and the Mac App Store may occasionally be shown to you based on your interests. Click the Ad button on the advertisement to find out why you were given that particular ad. To stop Apple from utilizing your information for ad targeting, you can disable personalized ads. You might still receive advertisements as a result of this, but they might be less pertinent to you. Navigate to System Settings > Privacy & Security, select Apple Advertising, and then disable Personalized Ads to stop them.

	Note: Following an authorization request from Apple News or Stocks to send you personalized advertisements, you will have the option to disable personalized adverts. Select About Apple Advertising & Privacy to read Apple's advertising and privacy policy.
Lockdown mode	If you think you are being personally targeted by a very sophisticated hack, limit the apps, websites, and services you use. Attacks like this rarely target the majority of people.

CHAPTER 12
MAINTENANCE AND ACCESSORIES

To guarantee your MacBook Air M4 lasts a long time and performs at its best, you must use the appropriate accessories and perform proper maintenance. A thorough guide on maintaining your gadget and the necessary add-ons that improve its functionality and preserve its worth can be found below. Your MacBook Air M4 will last for years if you take care of it with routine cleaning, software updates, and battery maintenance. Purchasing protective cases, extra storage, docking stations, and other accessories can greatly improve your MacBook Air M4's use and turn it into a productive and adaptable tool for work and play. You can get the most out of your MacBook Air M4's performance and longevity and make sure it works for you in a range of situations by adhering to these maintenance recommendations and selecting the right accessories.

Best Accessories for the MacBook Air M4

If you own a MacBook or are shopping for a MacBook user, you are undoubtedly aware that an at-home setup requires more than just a laptop and a stand. The correct MacBook accessories can help it store more data, charge more quickly at home or away from a power outlet, and avoid scuffs whether it's being used for work, play, or both. Apple's portable computers come with an extensive range of original and third-party peripherals, just like the iPhone and iPad. These items, which range from a USB-C hub with every port you could ever require to external storage that can keep up, will streamline your work at home and on the go.

Anker Prime Power Bank 20K

Whenever a power outlet is out of reach, use Anker's Prime 20K power bank to top off your phone if you or the person you're shopping for is always on the go. Its two USB-C connections may provide an additional workday's worth of screen time after just a few minutes of use, with an output of up to 100 watts, which is more than the typical charger of most Apple notebooks. Additionally, the portable battery pack can charge smaller or older devices because of its quick USB-A connector. In contrast to many competitors, the Prime 20K uses USB-C to quickly charge two devices at once without sacrificing performance. Sure, using all three ports will make one USB-C less powerful, but one will always be able to deliver the full 100 watts. Amazingly, charging the Prime's internal battery takes only as little time because its USB-C connectors can handle 100 watts of power. Throughout a week-long business trip, the battery pack performed admirably for me, keeping my 14-inch MacBook Pro and all other devices charged and ready. Its integrated color screen also lets me monitor the charging process and the battery's remaining capacity. This product is superior to high-capacity laptop battery packs from other manufacturers in terms of mobility, versatility, and speed. Anker also sells a larger, quicker Prime power bank with a higher capacity, in addition to a smaller model with two USB-C connectors.

Twelve South BookArc Flex Vertical MacBook Stand

If you want to use your MacBook as your desktop screen while using an external monitor, you should acquire the BookArc Flex stand. By retaining the notebook in clamshell mode, this useful accessory will conserve room for both you and the receiver of your gift. If you acquire one, cable clutter will also disappear because it's small enough to fit behind the majority of monitors. The Book Arc Flex's native compatibility with any MacBook impressed me. I like not having to worry about inserts and width changes to accommodate any version of Apple notebooks, as they differ in thickness when closed. You can use it with any Apple notebook, existing or future, thanks to its broad compatibility and simple setup.

Satechi On-The-Go Multiport Adapter

With this multiport USB-C adapter from Satechi, you may utilize your USB-C notebook with any outdated device you may use at home or work. It features an HDMI input, a gigabit ethernet port, two USB-A ports, two USB-C connectors (one for charging and one for high-speed data transfers), and, most amazingly, a VGA port. You can connect your brand-new notebook to projectors and displays that are decades old with the help of the last section. The stylish device also has a complete SD card reader in addition to a microSD card reader. I give Satechi a lot of credit for having two USB-C cables in the package. You may use the device anywhere and at any time thanks to one of them, which is neatly housed inside an integrated compartment in the adapter. I didn't have to worry about forgetting to take additional cords when I traveled because of this ingenious cable storage, which made gear organization easier. In my opinion, this is the greatest MacBook USB-C hub available, and I've been using one with multiple Apple computers since it was released. The space gray and black USB-C On-the-Go multiport converter from Satechi complements the hue of the MacBook.

Logitech MX Anywhere 3S Wireless Mouse

The greatest small wireless mouse available is the Logitech MX Anywhere 3S, which is also an excellent MacBook accessory. It features an extremely accurate stainless steel scrolling wheel with electromagnetic technology, as well as an ergonomic design and customizable buttons. Any surface, including glass, will function with it. Similar to its predecessor, the Logitech MX Anywhere 3S distinguishes itself from all competitors with its previously mentioned capacity to function dependably on any surface. I was able to utilize it with success on my living room couch, home dining table, and workplace desk. I saved time by scrolling through documents, spreadsheets, and online pages more quickly thanks to the device's sophisticated scrolling wheel. The device can easily switch between two PCs and pair with them. Its USB-C connector is used for charging, and its battery can go for months between charges. The MX Anywhere 3S is available in rose, graphite, and light gray color variants.

Anker Prime 100W USB-C Charger

Given that it is far more compact and multifunctional than the wall charger that comes with every MacBook, this moderately priced Anker wall charger is a great substitute. The device is also capable of speedier charging because of its one USB-C port, which can handle up to 100 watts of maximum charging output. The only 16-inch Pro adapter with a higher charging capacity is the considerably larger 140-watt model, yet I can attest that the Anker attachment can also juice up the big-screen notebook. Since 2022, I've been a fan of Anker's small three-port chargers, and the Prime 100W is the greatest one yet. I can always charge any gadget I have with me on the go thanks to its quick USB-C connections and flexible USB-A output. nker built advanced technology into the adapter to guard against overcharging and overheating the connected devices. If you're on a limited budget and looking for a MacBook-ready charger, have a look at this three-port option.

Native UnionFold Laptop Stand

The Native Union Fold MacBook stand is the ideal MacBook accessory to carry in your laptop backpack for on-the-go work if you depend on a stand for your laptop at home. Because it's the most basic product of its kind, it won't take up additional space in our bag and works with any MacBook. When working with your MacBook on a desk or any other flat surface, its 15-degree viewing angle will assist you in maintaining proper viewing posture. After using the Native Union Fold for a few weeks, I discovered that it was just as useful for using a MacBook Pro by itself or as a supplementary screen when connected to a desktop monitor. The understated stand was ideal for extended gaming sessions of Resident Evil 4 since it enhanced both the viewing angles and airflow of my MacBook. The attachment folds into a lightweight metal stick that is convenient to store in a wrapped pouch when not in use. The latter was really useful because it made it possible for me to store the stand next to my laptop without having to worry about scratching it.

Woolnut Leather and Wool MacBook Sleeve

This gorgeous MacBook sleeve by Woolnut was designed in Sweden and is made of real full-grain leather, making it both opulent and long-lasting. When you're not using your MacBook, its Scandinavian leather exterior will acquire a distinctive patina that will give it a charming and fashionable place to live. Given that the attachment is remarkably thin, you can fit it effortlessly inside the laptop section of a bag that contains a MacBook. It features a strong magnetic closure and a plush wool-felt interior lining to shield the notebook from scratches. Fortunately, the latter partially seals, allowing you to covertly charge your MacBook when needed. Given its sophisticated style and exceptional craftsmanship, the Woolnut leather sleeve is worth the high price. The product is available in brown, green, and black screen sizes for MacBooks.

Beats Studio Pro Wireless Headphones

For numerous reasons, the Beats Studio Pro wireless headphones are an ideal partner for a MacBook or other Apple device. It will be quite easy to switch between utilizing the cans with your MacBook, iPad, or iPhone because they will link to all Apple devices that share the same iCloud account. Naturally, the best headphones will also provide you with outstanding sound quality, robust noise cancellation, dynamic head tracking, and a long battery life. The fact that I could connect these headphones to my MacBook Pro via USB-C, Bluetooth, or a regular audio port is my favorite feature of them. My preferred option was the last one, which let me use the buttons on the left ear cup of the headphones to control the music and watch lossless content from Apple Music. I find it simple to choose the Beats Studio Pro over the AirPods Max these days because of its adaptability, included storage case, and 40-hour battery life. The well-known wireless cans are available in sandstone, navy, deep brown, and black.

Traveling and Using Your MacBook Air in Various Environments

Whether you're traveling for work or play, it's important to keep in mind how various circumstances can affect the longevity and performance of your MacBook Air. Here are some tips for protecting and using your MacBook Air in different scenarios.

Air Travel

- **Airport Security:** Prepare to take your MacBook Air out of your luggage so that it can be scanned by an X-ray machine when you go through security. To prevent scratches during handling, place it inside a protective case or sleeve.
- Use Your MacBook Air's small size and lengthy battery life for work or enjoyment while in flight. To prolong battery life during lengthy trips, go to low-power mode. To reduce background noise, think about utilizing AirPods or noise-canceling headphones.
- **Charging on the Go:** Make sure you have the right converter for the airline's power outlet if your flight has in-seat electricity. Bring a portable charger as a backup because low-voltage outlets might be available on some flights.

Outdoor Environments

- **Sunlight and Glare:** Screen glare can be a major problem when working outside. Set the brightness of your MacBook Air to its highest level and, if one is available, apply an antiglare screen protector. To lessen direct sunlight on the screen, look for areas that are shadowed.

- **Dust & Sand:** Use a keyboard cover and store your MacBook Air in a zippered case when not in use to protect it in dusty or sandy areas. Steer clear of using it in harsh environments where dust particles could get into the ports and harm the keyboard.
- **Temperature Extremes:** The 50° to 95° F or 10° to 35° C temperature ranges are intended for MacBook operation. Extreme heat or cold should not be allowed to touch your MacBook Air as this might harm internal components and lower battery life.

Remote Work and Co-Working Spaces

- **Wi-Fi and connectivity:** Make sure you have a dependable and safe Wi-Fi connection when working remotely or in a co-working place. To secure your data when using public networks, think about utilizing a VPN.
- **Ergonomics:** Even in temporary settings, arrange your workspace ergonomically. To keep your MacBook at eye level, use a portable laptop stand. To ensure a comfortable typing position, use an external keyboard and mouse.
- **Security:** Use Touch ID or enable a password to keep your MacBook Air safe when in public areas. Either carry your MacBook with you when you leave your workstation or secure it with a laptop lock to a stationary item.

Public Transport and Commuting

- **Portability and Compactness:** The MacBook Air's lightweight construction makes it the perfect device for commuters. Its solid-state drive guarantees that it can endure the bumps and jolts of travel, and its small design makes it easy to slip into most suitcases.
- **Privacy and Security:** Use a privacy screen to shield your screen from prying eyes and be aware of shoulder surfers when using public transportation. When not in use, always keep your MacBook Air in plain sight and store it safely.

Extreme Weather Conditions

High Humidity: Moisture can be an issue in tropical or humid regions. To absorb extra moisture, place packets of silica gel in the bag that holds your MacBook Air. When at all feasible, keep the MacBook in an air-conditioned space and avoid using it in very humid environments.

Rain & Water Exposure: When traveling in wet weather, always place your MacBook Air in a water-resistant bag or sleeve. If it becomes wet, turn it off right away, give it a thorough dry, and don't switch it on again until you're positive it's dry.

It takes preparation to travel with a MacBook Air, but if you take the necessary safety measures, you can make sure that your machine is safe, working, and prepared to help you wherever your travels take you. Your MacBook Air is a multipurpose friend that fits well in a variety of settings, be it negotiating airport security, working in a co-working space, or just spending a day outside. You can extend the life and performance of your MacBook Air by using these suggestions, which will make it an essential travel companion for business and play.

Cleaning and Maintaining Hardware

Maintaining and cleaning your MacBook Air M4 properly keeps it in top operating shape, increases its longevity, and helps ward off performance problems. This section will assist you in maintaining your device:

Constant cleaning of the Exterior

- **Microfiber Cloth**: To clean the outside of your MacBook Air, use a gentle, lint-free microfiber cloth. Refrain from using anything abrasive that might scratch the surface.
- **Damp Cloth**: Lightly moisten the cloth with water to remove stubborn smudges. Ensure that the towel is not excessively damp to prevent any liquid from leaking into the gadget.
- **Cleaning the Screen:** Use a fresh microfiber towel to gently wipe the screen. Use a screen cleaner made especially for electronics for more thorough cleaning, and make sure it doesn't contain ammonia or alcohol.

Keyboard and Ports Maintenance

- Compressed Air: Use a can of compressed air to clear the keyboard and ports of dust and dirt. Slightly tilt the MacBook so that you can spray brief spurts of air.
- Keyboard Cleaning: To give your keyboard a deeper clean, dab a microfiber cloth in water or a non-alcoholic cleaner, then lightly wipe off the keys. Steer clear of sprinkling liquid straight onto the keyboard.
- Cleaning the Ports: Use compressed air or a soft brush to carefully clean the ports. Take care not to harm the internal connectors.

Battery Care

- Avoid Extreme Temperatures: Because extremes in temperature can have an impact on the longevity and performance of batteries, keep your MacBook Air away from extremely hot or cold places.
- Frequent Use: Make sure the MacBook Air is used frequently and avoid leaving it plugged in all the time to preserve battery health. This aids in adjusting the charging cycle of the battery.
- Software Updates: Make sure the most recent macOS updates—which frequently feature enhancements for battery management—are installed on your MacBook Air.

Long-Term Storage

- Shut Down Correctly: Make sure your MacBook Air is shut down correctly if you intend to store it for a long time.
- Battery Storage: Keep the MacBook Air's battery charged to around 50% when storing it and check it every six months to see if it needs to be recharged. Keep the device away from places with a lot of humidity or heat.

Frequent cleaning, careful use, and appropriate storage techniques are all necessary to maintain the hardware of your MacBook Air M4. You can maintain your MacBook Air in top shape and make sure it continues to operate at its best for many years by adhering to these tips. Frequent maintenance helps avoid hardware problems that may result from misuse or negligence in addition to maintaining the device's aesthetic appeal.

Understanding AppleCare and Warranty Information

Verify whether your gadget is covered and find out what kind of maintenance and repairs are covered. Or locate the expiration date, proof of purchase, and agreement number.

- Navigate to **Settings > General > AppleCare & Warranty on your iPhone or iPad, then choose your device.**
- Choose the Apple menu in the lower left corner of your Mac screen. Choose **AppleCare & Warranty under System Settings > General.**
- Navigate to checkcoverage.apple.com and input your device's serial number. then adhere to the directions displayed on the screen.
- You can also check if your device is protected by visiting mysupport.apple.com. Select your device after logging in with your Apple ID.

See what your coverage includes and when your coverage expires

- Navigate to **Settings > General > AppleCare & Warranty on your iPhone or iPad, then choose your device.**
- Choose the Apple menu in the lower left corner of your Mac screen. Choose **AppleCare & Warranty under System Settings > General.**
- Enter your Apple ID to log in at mysupport.apple.com. Next, select your device to get information about the assistance, including technical help and hardware repairs, for which you qualify.

Obtain the agreement number or proof of coverage

- Go **to apple.com/mysupport.**

- Using **your Apple ID, log in.**
- Select **your gadget.**
- To see the Proof of Coverage, click on it. If your proof of coverage is not displayed, confirm that two-factor authentication is enabled for your Apple ID.

CHAPTER 13

TROUBLESHOOTING AND RECOVERY

Despite the MacBook Air M4's stellar performance and dependability reputation, problems may occasionally arise that call for troubleshooting or recovery procedures. The MacBook Air M4 requires a combination of software tools, maintenance procedures, and sometimes expert assistance for troubleshooting and recovery. Maintaining the functionality of your MacBook Air and reducing downtime can be achieved by knowing the fundamental procedures for identifying and fixing common problems. Being organized and aware of your device is essential to effectively resolve issues, whether you want to use Activity Monitor, Safe Mode, or Apple's built-in diagnostic tools. Maintaining storage and updating your software are two examples of regular maintenance that can help stop many problems before they start.

Reclaiming Space and Managing Updates

To get the best performance out of your MacBook Air M4, make sure you have enough storage space and that your software is up to date. Here are some pointers for effectively managing updates and freeing up space.

Reclaiming Space

Use storage management tools

- Optimize Storage: To help you make the most of your space, macOS comes with a built-in storage management tool. To access it, select **Manage from the Apple menu's Storage > About This Mac > menu**. This is where you activate features like "Store in iCloud," which automatically frees up local space by storing older files on iCloud.
- Reduce Clutter: You can evaluate and remove huge files, downloads, and unsupported apps that you no longer require by clicking the "Reduce Clutter" button in the same storage management interface.

Remove unused applications

- Uninstall Apps: Drag and drop programs you don't frequently use into the Trash folder from the Applications folder. To make sure that all related files are deleted, you can also use outside programs like AppCleaner.

Clear cache files

- Browser Caches: To free up space, frequently clear the cache in your web browsers, such as Safari. To delete website data, navigate to **Safari > Preferences**

Privacy > Manage Website Data.

- System Caches: Over time, system and application caches may fill up. To remove outdated cache files, either manually go to ~/Library/Caches or use programs such as CleanMyMac.

Manage large files

- Finder Search: To find huge files, use Finder's search feature. To find files greater than a specified size, open the Finder, hit Command + F, and adjust the search parameters. If these files are no longer needed, delete them or move them to an external device or cloud storage.

Managing Updates

Enable automatic updates

- System Updates: To guarantee you get the newest features and security updates, keep macOS and all of your programs up to date. Go to **Software Update under System Preferences, and then select "Automatically keep my Mac up to date."**
- App Updates: To enable automatic updates for apps downloaded from the App Store, **navigate to the App Store > Preferences menu and choose "Automatic Updates."**

Check for updates regularly

- Manual Check: It's a good idea to manually check for updates regularly, even when automatic updates are enabled. One way to accomplish this is to go to **System Preferences > Software Update or open the App Store and select "Updates."**
- Third-Party programs: To keep all of your software up to date, utilize tools like MacUpdate or frequently check the developer's website for updates if you don't get your programs from the App Store.

Free up space before major updates

- Backup Data: Make sure you have adequate free space and use Time Machine or another backup option to back up your data before installing any major macOS updates.

- Pre-Update Cleanup: Make sure your MacBook has enough space to run the update without any problems by removing huge files, unused programs, and temporary files.

Backing Up and Recovering Files

Discover how to back up the files on your Mac.

Use Time Machine to back up automatically

Your Mac comes with an integrated backup feature called Time Machine. Apps, music, pictures, emails, documents, and other types of media can all be automatically backed up using Time Machine using a USB stick or other storage device. Then, you can restore your files—older files, deleted files, and files that are no longer accessible—using your backup.

Backup your Mac with Time Machine

Apps, music, pictures, emails, documents, and other types of media can all be automatically backed up using Time Machine to an external storage device, such as a USB drive.

Connect a storage device to your Mac

Attach an external storage device, like a Thunderbolt or USB disk.
- Make use of a storage device that has twice the amount of storage space as your Mac. Your backup drive should preferably contain at least 2 TB of storage if, for instance, your Mac only has 1 TB of storage. Time Machine will notify you if it needs additional storage on your Mac.
- Don't use your Time Machine backup disk to store other data; only use it for backups.

Set up the storage device as your backup disk

- Select **System Settings from the Apple menu located in the corner of your screen.**
- Select **General from the sidebar, and then select Time Machine from the list on the right.**
- Either click the **Add button (+) or select Add Backup Disk.**
- Click **Set up Disk after selecting the connected storage device.**
- **While everything is being set up:**
  - To use the storage device for Time Machine, your Mac can ask if you wish to wipe it. Either remove it or choose an alternative backup volume or disk.
  - Your Mac might inquire as to whether it is the right computer to take ownership of backups that were made on another one. If you would like the backups to be included in this Mac's backups, you must claim them.

Your Mac will begin using the storage disk for backups as soon as the setup is complete.

Make a backup

Select Backup Now from the Time Machine menu to start a backup right away. There is no alt for the image in the navigation bar. Or hold off until the subsequent automated backup. To check the status of a backup or to stop or skip it, use the same menu. The date and time of the most recent backup, or the percentage of the current backup that has been completed, are displayed at the top of the menu.

Backup frequency and duration

Time Machine creates backups automatically every hour for the last twenty-four hours, every day for the last thirty days, and every week for the last sixty days. When your backup drive is full, the oldest backups will be removed.

- Select **Open Time Machine Configuration** from the Time Machine menu to modify the backup frequency on macOS Ventura or later. There is no alt provided for the image. Select **an option from the "Backup frequency" menu by clicking Options**.

Although the initial backup could take longer than anticipated, you can keep using your Mac throughout this time. Future backups will be speedier since Time Machine only backs up files that have changed since the last backup.

Sync and Store data with iCloud

Moreover, you may use iCloud to sync and access data on all of your devices that have the same Apple ID registered in iCloud. Your contacts, calendars, notes, movies, passwords, and much more are safe, automatically backed up, and accessible from anywhere with iCloud.

- Log into your iCloud account.
- To configure which of your apps synchronize and retain information with iCloud, go to the iCloud settings.
- You can save other files in iCloud, including those in your Documents and Desktop folders, by using iCloud Drive.

Your iCloud storage plan's storage capacity will be depleted by storing files there. If your iCloud storage is full, you may either purchase additional iCloud storage straight from your Apple device or increase the amount of storage that is available. To have an additional duplicate of the data kept in iCloud, you can also archive or create copies of it.

Resolving macOS Crashes and Issues

Your MacBook Air M4 macOS crashes and problems can be fixed with a methodical approach that starts with simple troubleshooting and progresses to more sophisticated techniques as needed. You can maintain a dependable and stable system by updating your applications, managing disk space wisely, and knowing when to reset or reinstall macOS. If everything else fails, Apple offers expert support that can help you restore your MacBook Air's optimal performance.

Identifying the cause of the crash

Finding the source of a macOS crash is the first step towards fixing it. Typical reasons include:

- Software Conflicts: Outdated or incompatible apps may be the reason behind a macOS crash. Making sure all of your software is current and works with the macOS version you are using is crucial.
- Hardware Problems: Unstable systems can result from malfunctioning hardware, including RAM or external peripherals. Take into consideration taking out or replacing any new hardware you may have installed recently to see if that fixes the problem.
- System File Corrupted: Crashes may result from corrupted system files or configurations. This could happen following a system update or if macOS isn't able to correctly read important files.
- Low Disk Space: When macOS has insufficient disk space, it may crash or become unresponsive. Make sure you have enough free space so that macOS runs smoothly.

Basic troubleshooting steps

Start by following these simple instructions to fix common macOS problems:

- **Restart Your Mac**: A quick restart can frequently resolve short-term issues and free up RAM. Navigate to the Apple menu and choose "Restart" to restart.
- Verify that all installed apps and macOS are current by checking for updates. To check for macOS updates, navigate to **System Preferences > Software Update**. To update your apps, open the App Store and select **"Updates"**.
- **Safe Mode:** Selecting Safe Mode at Mac startup can assist in determining the crash's origin. Restart your Mac, then hold down the Shift key until the login screen shows to enter Safe Mode. Safe Mode might assist you in figuring out whether third-party software is the source of the issue by disabling unnecessary starting components.
- Make sure you have adequate free disk space by checking your disk space. To view the available space, navigate to the **Apple menu > About This Mac**

> **Storage.** Consider removing or shifting unwanted data to an external device if there is not enough space.

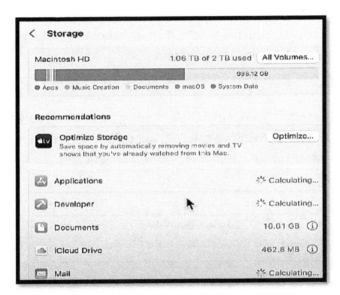

Advanced Troubleshooting

If standard troubleshooting doesn't work, you might need to use more sophisticated techniques:

- **Reset NVRAM/PRAM:** Your Mac's startup settings are stored in NVRAM (Non-Volatile Random-Access Memory). Resetting NVRAM/PRAM can occasionally assist if you're having crashes. Restart your Mac, and then hold down the Option, Command, P, and R keys for approximately 20 seconds to reset.

- **Reset the System Management Controller (SMC)**: Your Mac's SMC regulates low-level operations including heat control and power management. Resetting the SMC can assist in resolving hardware, fan, or power-related problems. On a MacBook Air with a non-removable battery, to reset the SMC, turn off your computer, press and hold the **Shift, Control, and Option keys on the left side of the keyboard, and simultaneously click the power button. After holding down all keys for ten seconds, restart your Mac.**
- **Launch Disk Utility:** To fix your starting disk, use Disk Utility. Restart your Mac, hold **Command + R to boot into macOS Recovery,** and use Disk Utility. To search for and fix disk issues, select Disk Utility, select your **startup disk, and click "First Aid".**
- **Use Activity Monitor:** To determine whether any particular programs are sucking up too much resources or triggering the crash, open **Activity Monitor (located under Applications > Utilities)**. You can force terminate a misbehaving process via Activity Monitor if you discover one.

Reinstalling MacOS

It can be necessary for you to reinstall macOS if troubleshooting is unable to fix the problem. You can accomplish this without erasing your data:

- Make a backup of your data using Time Machine or another backup tool before reinstalling macOS.
- To reinstall macOS, restart your computer and enter macOS Recovery by holding down the **Command + R key. Select "Reinstall macOS" and adhere to the prompts displayed on the screen.** This will restore macOS without erasing any of your files.

Conclusion

The MacBook Air M4 is a strong, effective, and adaptable gadget that perfectly captures Apple's dedication to user experience and innovation. This laptop is the ideal combination of portability and performance, whether you're an experienced professional wanting to upgrade or a novice just entering the Mac environment. The MacBook Air M4, with its cutting-edge M4 CPU, gorgeous Retina display, and smooth macOS integration, is designed to tackle a wide range of tasks, from routine office work to strenuous creative projects.

INDEX

www.ingramcontent.com/pod-product-compliance
Lightning Source LLC
La Vergne TN
LVHW081342050326
832903LV00024B/1264